Also from R.S. Amblee

The Audacity of Futurism

Winner at 2017 National Indie Excellence Awards

First prize at 2017 Los Angeles Book Festival

Runner-up at 2017 Amsterdam Book Festival

THE UGLY FIGHT

UNLEASHING ARTIFICIAL INTELLIGENCE AGAINST GLOBAL WARMING

R.S. Amblee

In the middle of difficulty lies opportunity.

– Albert Einstein

■ Contents

Introduction: Propitious Time for Artificial Intelligence　　3

■ *Part I: The Plan*　　5

Chapter 1: What Is AI Anyway?　　7

Chapter 2: Is It Global Warming or Climate Change?　　35

Chapter 3: The Plan to Unleash AI　　47

■ *Part II: The Epic Battle*　　51

Chapter 4: The Defiant Global Heat　　53

Chapter 5: Capture That Carbon　　61

Chapter 6: Soliciting the Solar　　77

Chapter 7: The Face of Victory　　95

■ *Part III: Collateral Damage*　　99

Chapter 8: Men Not at Work　　101

Chapter 9: Print a Roof Overhead　　105

Chapter 10: Reinventing Transportation 113

Chapter 11: Inventively Serving Food 131

Chapter 12: Intelligent Care of Health 137

Epilogue: 157

Bibliography 163

Index 171

The Ugly Fight

Propitious Time for Artificial Intelligence

I suppose this book started when I delved deeply into the unfathomable artificial intelligence (AI). The world of AI seemed so grandiose that I was simply lost in it. AI is pretty much in every facet of our economy: energy, manufacturing, food, healthcare, transportation, and even house construction. Just out of curiosity I began to explore AI's capabilities to fight global warming, and to my surprise I found many techniques were already in the arena but at an insignificantly small scale.

Pragmatically, to fight global warming we need a gargantuan amount of ecological big data and an intelligence that can unravel its complexities. Both prerequisites are at their infancy stage. We do not have much ecological data as of now and the capability of AI, which invariably depends on this data, is naturally stunted.

So far we have not made any noticeable progress, not a dent. Global temperatures are still on the rise. Hurricanes are becoming bigger and stronger and destructive floods and draught are becoming a way of life.

Artificial intelligence is one of the more colossal innovations ever conceived by humanity. Global warming is an unruly beast from the slipshod world. When you look at these two mighty forces, they are completely diametric. While global warming has the potential to destroy our ecosystem, AI has the potential to protect it. It's not hard to envision a solution brewing right in front of our eyes.

But AI is a double-edged sword. When we nurture AI to fight global warming, undoubtedly it will threaten our jobs. Now the challenge is not just to combat climate change but to survive the collateral damage. It is an ugly fight indeed. And I found AI has amazing potential to foster the unemployed.

I have done my best to bring all the current global endeavors under one roof giving the AI a form, a shape and a voice, so the world would recognize its importance and start using it as a strategy and not just as a tool.

PART I

THE PLAN

Chapter 1

What Is AI Anyway?

***Artificial intelligence**: the intelligence exhibited by self-learning software. It is also the name of the academic field of study that is becoming main stream and has a career path.*

This chapter explores AI and its practical applications in the real world with noteworthy examples. The next chapter details how global warming is feeding on itself and is spinning out of control. The third and last chapter in this part-I lays out a detailed plan to fight global warming by harnessing AI's capability.

The buzzword artificial intelligence (AI) has really fascinated the world. While humans are still early in understanding human intelligence, they have the audacity to build an artificial intelligence!

Being in the IT industry myself for more than two decades, my fascination with this new software kept growing as it became more widespread every day. It's just unbelievable that this weird term that made its academic appearance recently already has a career path in its name. I began to wonder if all the hype was undue attention because it sounds so cutting edge or if it was because AI has true value. I started my own reconnoiter out of unquenchable curiosity. The more I dug, the more captivating I found it.

When it comes to understanding computer programs, there is nothing equivalent to wetting our hands. So I started to learn AI by coding it. I coded a self-driving virtual car that sniffs around and finds its way to the destination with the shortest route. After all the hard work and finally completing the python code, a small, ant-like bug began to crawl on my computer screen going all over in random directions. That was my AI algorithm!

Why was it crawling all around, you may ask. Because the start and end positions were not specified yet. Amazingly, when I keyed in the start and end positions, this little creature slowly changed its course, and instead of moving randomly it began to move around the starting position for a while and then it crawled toward the end position. Once it reached the end position, after maybe ten or fifteen back and forth movements, it learned the quickest way to move between those two points. However, even though it found the shortest way to reach the destination it did not give up its habit of sniffing around to find potential shorter routes to eliminate any possibility of taking a longer route.

That constant sniffing gives AI the special ability to learn from its own mistakes just like humans do. It was just an incredible experience. It's not a typical software that obediently follows the hard rules; this was an ever-learning software. What was moving like an ant all around the screen now began to look more like a commuter car between downtown and the airport. Software that learns on its own!

In my career as an IT professional, I am used to giving commands to software to do tasks for a specific result. I had never written software that could act on its own to achieve a specific result. It changed my perception of AI forever. So I started learning more about this amazing human creation.

You may be wondering how this software learned the shortest route. The simplest explanation is, it's coded in such a way that the behavior of the bug is dependent on what is called a reward point. Every time the bug moves closer to the destination, it gets a reward point. Every time the bug moves away from the destination, it loses a point. The goal of this computer program is to bag as many rewards as possible.

How does it know which way it has to move to get closer without GPS or any direction sensor? It uses a heuristic technique—essentially trial and error—to compute the distance. That data is then automatically stored in a memory matrix. That's why it initially goes in random directions before finally computing the most optimal way. This computation of optimal path is called training for the AI, a process that is highly CPU intensive. This unique learning capability is the reason it's becoming so powerful and the darling of the world.

A heuristic technique is not the only one used in AI. There are tons of them, and they are not new. These are age-old ideas and mathematical models that were never tested on computers because they were dead-slow in previous decades. Now with faster computers, it's no surprise old concepts are being rediscovered.

Another popular AI technique is called artificial neural networks or simply neural net (NN). This is one of the top-notch techniques modeled after the neural structure of the human brain. The disparity is that NN might use a few hundred neurons, whereas the neural structure of the human brain has approximately one hundred billion neurons. It's obvious that humans have a better capability with things like face, object, voice, and natural language recognition as well as many more complex qualities that machines don't have yet. However, NN has the capability to outpace human neural networks very quickly as it takes only a few more central processing units (CPUs)—popularly called chips—and few more gigabits of memory to add more neurons. The truth is the capability of NN is boundless.

Now let's look at the structure of a human neural network a bit more closely from the perspective of data flow. In human brains every neuron is connected to a bunch of other neurons. Obviously, the output of one neuron becomes the input to other neurons, meaning the signal coming from one neuron is captured by other neurons connected to it as their source of information. Based on multiple inputs, a neuron generates a new output that can be used again as input to other neurons. This goes on like a crazy maze in these one hundred billion neurons.

The basic idea here is the strength of input signals decides the output signal from a neuron. If a neuron is getting high-strength signals from all its inputs, its output will be influenced by the strong signals. If you touch a hot plate by accident, all the nerve endings on the hand will send out strong signals to the brain, which cause the brain to act, and your hand is pulled back as a reflex action almost before you are aware of it. The brain processes the inputs and acts on them based purely on the strength or weakness of the signals. The same technique has been adapted in NN. Furthermore, each artificial neuron is designed to use a mathematical function to determine its own output.

Here is an example of the object recognition capability of NN. Let's say you have a basket of random objects and you want AI to recognize them. In reality NN doesn't know a thing about any object in the basket. When you show AI an object like a toy bird, the camera image of the bird is broken by the NN into a number of individual images. Each image is fed to a different neuron that gives its own weight to the image based on its own calculations.

Some of these images could be very prominent features for identification, while others may not be. For instance, the beak is a prominent feature to identify a bird. As NN are not initially aware of these prominent features, it gives random weight for their prominence. Discernibly, the prediction would be random too. If the prediction is incorrect, then weights are readjusted. This happens over and over again until the NN learn all the features that are useful for identification. It will eventually determine which features of the bird are more prominent. The more you train NN, the closer they get to the right answer.

After training, when a photo of a new bird is shown, the NN will give its best answer. The accuracy of the answer depends on the volume and variations of the data that was fed during training. In other words the quality of data matters. If there is a weird bird that is confusing to the human eye, AI might also falter if that kind of data is not in the database and was not fed in during the training.

Obviously, if you show the image of an elephant to the bird-trained AI, it won't know what it is because it would need specific training on elephants. You can't possibly train AI on every species, so this is where big data comes in. If the information about an animal is available in a database, fully identified and tagged, then the AI can skim thru the database and learn from it instantly.

The Blast of Big Data

Every min about three million messages are posted on Facebook, fifty thousand pictures are shared, half a million tweets tweet out, and forty million texts zip out. Every time we shop, we spawn tons of data tied to banks, retailers, and industries. This mountain of data is given a name: big data. The blast of big data is so huge it is humanly impossible even for professionals to make sense of it. This level of complexity and volume of data gave birth to software like data analytics tools that extract, analyze, and interpret data in a way that is useful to us.

However, no matter how sophisticated the data analytics software is, it has limited capability and will only do exactly what it is coded for. Big data has innumerable data patterns hidden in it, and it's not possible to code software to unearth all the individual combinations. This was when AI emerged as a natural solution to pull meaningful information out of big data. AI can identify observable patterns and predict things without having explicit pre-programmed rules and models.

For example, if you want to know what city has more crime, a simple database query can figure it out, or a simple data analytics tool can answer that instantly. However, if you want to know what specific locality is going to get hit by a criminal gang in the next twenty-four hours, you have to go thru numerous data sources such as Facebook postings, tweets, texts, Google searches, local demographics and criminal reports—zillions of data points. It would be humanly impossible to concoct all this structured and unstructured data and predict a pattern of criminal acts. It's like looking for a needle in a haystack. You need an AI that correlates this massive data in a useful way.

To find those hidden patterns, AI is trained to predict some past events that have already occurred based on past data. If it makes a mistake, it reevaluates and predicts again, learning iteratively over and over again until it becomes a useful tool. How well AI predicts depends on the quality of data. Garbage in, garbage out is appropriate here. The quality of big data is as important as skillfully coded AI itself. If you want AI to predict anything, the data has to be vast, varied, high-quality, and as real-time as feasible.

Broadly speaking, there are two kinds of data sources: human generated and machine-generated. Human-generated data includes social media, blogs, Google search, texting, tweeting, online shopping, and so on. Though these data sources appear humungous, they eventually flatten out because data caused by human activity can't be infinite as humans can only do finite things in a day. The data growth seems mammoth because more and more people are gaining access to the Internet every day and once all seven billion people on the planet become part of the global digital community we will have reached a level of stability in data generation.

The only data that will continue to grow unabated is machine data. Machines are all around us and continue to grow in number as the economy expands. These machines will be more useful to us if they generate valuable information. Most machines generate data via the Internet of Things (IoT).

The Internet of Things in Real Life

IoTs are phenomenal entities as they feed vital data to AI. In today's world any digital device that connects to the Internet is termed a smart device. All smart devices—smart watches, smart garage doors, smart TVs, smart refrigerators—are IoTs. Any gadget can be made smart by giving it the capability to connect to the Internet. A device cannot be an IoT, no matter how sophisticated it is, if it is not able to connect to the Internet. The reason for emphasizing an Internet connection is that it gives the device a unique identity in the digital world. We call this unique ID an Internet protocol (IP) address. Every computer in the world today has an IP address. An IoT can't connect to the Internet unless it has an IP address.

Say you have a smart refrigerator, which can do many things like inform you when the milk is empty, when the eggs are gone, and so on. These capabilities come from the IoT sensors. The milk sensor is set up to know the weight of the milk carton. When you place your milk carton at the designated spot, the sensor will measure the weight of the milk and send the data to the IoT. In essence, an IoT is an agent between its sensors and the Internet. A more apt definition is that an IoT is a smart chip that constantly captures data via its sensors. It's a device meant to feed AI with vital data.

In the smart refrigerator, similarly, the egg sensor sends weight of the eggs. The IoT chip in turn captures and sends out data to your phone app via the Internet. And your phone app driven by AI will do whatever it is configured to do. Maybe it will beep or send a text or email to you. It may even order milk if you have set it up that way. From this IoT data AI learns your usage pattern and advises you improving your lifestyle immeasurably.

Today's smart homes are filled with IoTs. From room thermostats all the way to garbage bins there are IoTs. In smart homes AI needs a lot of data to learn and become a useful tool. For instance, if you want AI to prepare coffee when you wake up or to switch off the lights and close the garage when you leave the house or even to start the furnace and keep the house warm before you arrive, AI needs data to learn your lifestyle. IoTs brew mammoth amount of data for AI. While IoT is a data producer AI is a data analyzer. This interdependency is what makes them a powerful duo to fight global warming that we are going to discuss in upcoming chapters.

Here is an invigorating example to show how city administrations could use our home IoTs to save energy. Say it is an exceptionally hot summer day and the power utility company is experiencing blackouts. When customers lose power, the utility staff can spend hours or days fixing the problem and dealing with angry customers. In an IoT world, this can be entirely different. The utility staff could quickly react to avert a blackout by turning everyone's thermostat up five degrees. A good AI could even alert the utility staff to an impending blackout. Or the AI itself could proactively turn thermostats up five degrees at all smart homes and non-essential businesses, leaving temperature-sensitive facilities such as hospitals and refrigerated warehouses alone. IoT and AI can do wonders if they are harnessed efficiently.

Here is a good example of IoT in healthcare. Say a patient is remotely monitored with a wearable device and the heart rate increases to an unsafe level. The IoT senses the data in real-time and transmits it. This data has to be analyzed, and the abnormalities need to be identified. If this responsibility is assigned to an individual who is monitoring patients remotely, reviewing data from thousands of patients in real-time is impossible. Even coding software with rules is time-consuming and fraught with errors. This is where AI comes in. It analyzes data in real time as it gets collected and flags anything outside the norm. This data sharing between AI and IoT is lifesaving.

IoTs around the world are producing a treasure trove of machine data on traffic, weather, crime, healthcare, supermarkets, industrial robotics, smart homes, and so on. AI is taking advantage of big data and is evolving, and its capabilities are all-encompassing: sales projections, crime prediction, weather forecasting, object, face, language, and voice recognition, and even playing chess!

The RFID Riddle

It is worth discussing radio frequency identification (RFID) as it coexists with IoTs in many places. RFID is a digital barcode (a microchip). The difference is that in a bar code the data is static, it can't be updated. In an RFID system data can be updated. RFID tags are good for storing vital information like expiration date, manufacturing date, package destination, and so on.

The RFID tags or microchips can be attached to objects like an automobile during production to track its progress through the assembly line. The RFID-tagged pharmaceutical products are very popular now-a-days. RFID tags can even be in used in livestock and pets for their identification and tracking.

As RFID tags do not have the capability to connect to the Internet, they have very little value without IoTs. To understand the usefulness of RFID, let's take the example of the smart refrigerator again. Say you bought a carton of milk with an RFID tag and stored it in your smart refrigerator. The RFID reader in the refrigerator reads the tag and sends its expiration date to the IoT in the refrigerator which in turn sends it to your phone app via Internet. However, RFID can't sense the weight of the milk carton and hence can't send you information about how much milk is still left in the carton. RFID can only give static data and not dynamic data as it is not a sensor.

RFID existed well before IoTs came into the market. They are gaining more importance in today's logistic world as they feed vital data to IoTs.

RFIDs can cost anywhere from a few cents to several dollars depending on the size and range of data transmittal. They can be as small as postage stamps or as big as your car transponder. RFID application is quite widespread in credit cards, hotel room cards, car keys, car transponders, passports, ID cards, driver license cards—they are pretty much everywhere.

RFID reader can simultaneously read several hundred tags. The RFID reader can hang from the ceiling and read all the tags in the warehouse and send the inventory list to an IoT. As RFIDs are not connected to the Internet, an IoT makes an RFID come to life.

RFID technology is very useful in warehouses to track inventory. Even trucks are attached with RFID. As they go from one warehouse to another, they are read and tracked. Many cars have RFID transponders that can be used in tollways and parking lots to open the gates. Any object can be tagged with RFID: key chains, wallets, bicycles, pets, and even hospital patients. RFID is very useful in pharmacies to manage inventory. Soon you will see express checkouts where your shopping cart is instantly scanned eliminating customers having to hand scan items.

Data security is a major issue as RFID can give out our secrets. Say you bought an expensive Rolex watch; the RFID tag on the watch could be broadcasting it as you walk down the street. A smart thief can figure it out. These kinds of security issues are being ironed out.

There are also some technical problems to address. Since RFID uses radio frequencies, it can jam when using overlapping frequencies. This could be life-threatening in a hospital. RFID readers are prone to collision issues when signals overlap. However, anti-collision protocols are being developed to counter that. The bottom line is technical challenges are not showstoppers; they only make the system better. Amid all the technical limitations, RFID has become an extended arm for IoTs to capture data.

The take away from this discussion is that IoTs and RFID are like eyes or ears for AI to make decisions. Whenever you hear the words big data, remember IoTs and RFID is where most, if not all, of the machine data will be coming from.

Amazon Go, the innovative new shopping technology is going one step ahead. Customers can shop and leave the store without having to stop and pay. Each Amazon Go store is fitted with hundreds of cameras that track items customers put in their bags, then add the item to their online shopping cart. If the customer puts the item back onto the shelf, it's removed from their virtual basket. Then when they leave the store, their chosen payment method is charged. Amazon Go's technology does not use chips to tag the items. Until such chip-less technologies become mainstream, RFID will rule the world of big data.

Now let's explore some interesting AI applications we have in the market today. With each of these examples, give your best thoughts to diagnose what jobs might disappear and what new opportunities could pop up and what skills we may need to grab them early on.

AI in Movies

The entertainment industry is going to hit $800 billion soon. It's a massive industry and is undoubtedly attracting AI to streamline the movie-making process to give audiences more bang for their buck.

Recently a movie trailer was produced by AI. IBM Watson (AI software) created a ten-minute trailer for the movie *Morgan*. Watson went through the movie and selected a few emotional movements of love, hate, anger, and horror then made a few short clippings for the director to choose from. (To see the trailer, Google AI Morgan trailer; it's enthralling to watch.) AI not only saved millions of dollars, it also introduced its own machine ideas, surprising even the creators of AI, which is still bad at reading human emotion but is getting better.

Similar attempts are going on in Japan. McCann Erickson Japan introduced a new AI "creative director" named AI-CD ß that made a commercial for Clorets mints. The AI was given a decade's worth of commercial ads to learn from. Though AI has not been fully established in the film industry, it's at the doorstep. (To see its ad, Google AI-CD beta.)

AI in Sports

IBM Watson has entered Wimbledon. Its video software uses crowd noise, social traction, facial recognition, and sentiment analysis of players to generate automated video highlights. So a video editor will no longer need to cut and edit to put a highlights package together.

AI in Chatbots

Chances are you already have some sort of chatty virtual assistant or chatbot: Alexa, SIRI, GoogleNow, Cortana, and so on. Amazon's Alexa sits inside each Echo speaker. Apple's SIRI runs on iPhones and understands multiple ways of asking questions, so you don't need to worry about remembering exact phrasing for commands. Google Now in Android systems knows your commute, your interests, and details about your daily schedule. It is loaded with predictive features. Microsoft's Cortana is great for location-based reminders. Most e-commerce websites are chat enabled.

Companies train these chatbots—literally chat robots—before putting them live for customers to use. During training they use most frequently used questions and relevant answers creating an answer bank. However, if the question that a customer asks is outside of the answer bank, then it will either give an irrelevant answer or a totally wrong answer. However, if they are AI-assisted, then they would learn every time you chat with them.

These chatbots you buy listens to you, observes your behavior, learns about you every time you tweet, watch a movie, listen to music, Google searches and do online purchases. As it learns, it serves more efficiently. This may look more like an invasion of privacy, but that is what the world chose.

Here is a simple litmus test to see if the chatbot that claims to be AI really is or not. Ask the virtual assistant some sample questions and note the responses. If you repeatedly ask these questions over a certain period of time, maybe few weeks or months, and the answer is the same, most probably it is not yet using AI. On the other hand, if this gadget is learning about you and is giving you a more useful response each time, then in all probability it could be using some sort of AI.

Two-Day Product Delivery

Major retailers do purchase prediction. Most of the time when you browse for a product, the AI in their websites identify you as a potential customer and email you special offers. They can send you coupons, offer you discounts, and target you with advertisements while also stocking their warehouses that are close to you with products that you're likely to buy. That is how your product is delivered the next day.

Product delivery is becoming smarter and beginning to look more like fire stations servicing specific areas. They need to get to the fire within a specific time frame, so stations are strategically located throughout the city. A similar system is being used in product delivery, which is why Amazon has been building warehouses all over the United States. Each warehouse services a specific area, and the AI knows the needs of that population, so each warehouse is uniquely stocked to cater to a specific demographic population. Likewise, when customers browse for products online, AI knows which products will be in the greatest demand during the coming holiday season and stocks accordingly. All these decisions need a lot of data and analytics in real-time done every min of the day. AI is built to make these decisions and constantly learn from its mistakes.

AI in Humanoids

The robot Sophia is a social humanoid created by Hong Kong-based Hanson Robotics. Sophia was activated on April 19, 2015. This robot imitates human gestures and facial expressions. It can answer questions on certain predefined topics. This humanoid is designed to be a conversational companion for people in retirement communities, hospitals, and nursing homes. It is also capable of entertaining crowds thru social conversation. This humanoid is on YouTube, and it's captivating to watch the facial expressions on this robot.

The AI algorithm was designed by SingularityNET, which aims to foster an open market for AIs.

AI in Policing

The American company ShotSpotter has developed a technology to help identify gunshots. It has placed sensors in most tall buildings in cities, and when a gun is fired, these sensors capture the sound and vibrations and mutually exchange data to pinpoint the exact location of the gunshot and alert the police. This is not only saving lives but also reducing the time and effort to respond, eventually reducing the cost.

Another interesting twist comes from a US company called Predpol which can detect crime before it happens. They look at past history and figure out the crime trend and identify potential areas and possible time of day. Though they can't predict exact location or exact time, their predictions would help police be on alert in those targeted during a specified window of time saving life, time, and money.

The Chinese company Hikvision uses video surveillance cameras to read license plates, use facial recognition, and even detect unattended bags in crowded areas and alert law enforcement officers.

Another Chinese company Cloud Walk is going one step ahead. It is using facial recognition software to identify suspicious and unusual body language that could trigger a security alert. Machines are not only learning but saving data on those individuals to help AI evolve to counter crime.

AI in Recruiting

Are you looking for a job right now or likely to look for one in the near future? Chances are you will be interacting with a virtual assistant most likely driven by AI. This AI may concern you because it learns a lot about you and stores all that data digitally, so your profile will be available to all potential employers.

Employers should also be equally concerned as their profile will also be available to all potential candidates. If the employer is racially biased, it will show up in the recruitment history.

You can't avoid this route. So be prepared to face this digital challenge and be attentive to what you give out. Since you will be interfacing with a machine instead of a human, it could be a new experience. You may ask the wrong questions or give the wrong answers to AI. Everything is digitally recorded.

One fascinating thing that has happened to the recruitment process is that biases are slowly being extinguished. The AI software scans through the résumés of potential candidates without considering gender, age, and name to eliminate biases that could steer the focus away from promising candidates. It also flags missing information from the résumés that the employer is looking for.

When candidates apply for a job, even before the résumés reaches the employer, AI-driven software will communicate with candidates not only to collect more information and do prescreening tests but also to share employer information. This helps the candidates as well by knowing if they are looking at the right employer before attending any further face-to-face interviews to avoid wasting time for both. Employers love this approach. Remember; the fundamental approach has not changed. To effectively prescreen the candidates, AI asks challenging questions and looks for effective answers.

Many recruiting AIs are becoming proactive and going one step further in compiling a list of potential candidates not currently in the job market but who may seek employment in the future. AI can identify which candidate would be likely to change jobs because of a company merger or layoffs. Also if a candidate updates their LinkedIn profile, it's a sign that the candidate could be looking for a new job.

Hiring is now popularly referred to as talent acquisition. There are plenty of talent acquisition companies like LinkedIn, Indeed, Glassdoor, Dice, Monster, Craigslist, Plaxo, Jobster, and so on. There are also many companies that are developing talent acquisition software like Ideal, Avrio, Entelo, Engage Talent, Paradox Olivia, and Mya Systems. You may visit their sites to learn how they are developing and using AI to acquire talent. These companies focus on developing machine learning software to mediate between candidates and the employers.

AI in the Stock Market

Picking promising stocks every day is arduous for portfolio managers and needs a lot of proficient people. They have to scan data coming from news media, social media, blogs, company announcements, consumer confidence reports, real-time volatility in the stock market, etc. The amount of data is so exhaustive it is implausible to analyze and arrive at fortune stocks to invest in. This is where machine learning is picking up steam.

The US company Kavout is engaged in building deep learning algorithms to assist individuals in trading. People can now hire AI instead of humans for trading.

This company also uses sentiment analysis, which looks at how people, traders, investors, company CEOs, and others react to any stock market news. The AI is using all this data to make good investment decisions.

AI is also influencing algorithmic trading and high-frequency trading systems. Many robot advisors are in the market today. Most hedge funds and financial institutions have their own version of AI.

As you can see the data is so vast and varied, that the AIs of different companies analyze them in different ways. So there is competition to build the best AI for the stock market. The race is on; the winners are the individuals like us. Skilled jobs are plenty in this ever-inflating financial industry.

AI still needs babysitting in many ways, as any software glitch could wipe out portfolios. The computer glitch of 2012 has left a bad taste in everyone's mouth. Although AI is threatening the traditional portfolio management jobs, the financial market still needs people who can understand both AI and business at the same time. Portfolio managers have to learn to live with AI, which offers both a job threat and job opportunities at the same time.

AI in Rescue Operations

Do you know there are unique robots that look like and act like animals? For example, eMotion Butterfiles from the company Festo fly like real ones. Their dragonfly-like BionicOpter robots fly and glide in the air. Their bionic ants are the size of a hand. Their AquaPenguin can swim in water, look, and act like real penguins. Their bionic kangaroo looks like and jumps like a real kangaroo. There are captivating videos online that are worth watching.

The Defense Advanced Research Projects Agency (DARPA), a wing of the US Department of Defense, has created a variety of incredible robots. It's riveting to watch these robots in action on YouTube videos.

These amazing machines are a blessing in disguise for disaster response. They can fly, crawl, or walk into places humans can't. They can operate in environments where humans can't even survive. During disasters like hurricanes, tornadoes, floods, forest fires, nuclear leakages, and earthquakes they bring data of immense value. While some of them can collect data others can help in real rescue operations.

Future rescue is all about AI-driven intelligent, quick-witted, canny robots. Though AI is being blamed for taking away our jobs, if you look at the quality of services it is providing and how much value it is adding to society, we can only cherish the technology.

AI in Robotics

Regrettably robots have a very limited number of sensors, and therefore a very limited amount of data is fed to the robot brain. Most of the robotic movements are using limited incoming data. No wonder robots are very limited in their capability. Compare this to the human body. For instance, the skin that covers the human body is filled with trillions of nerve endings. You touch the skin with a needle, and you will not find one single area that can't sense it unless you have a skin disease.

Now imagine filling the robotic body with such a vast number of sensors, generating a prodigious amount of data at a staggering rate. No hard-coded software can handle such a mammoth amount of data. You need a brain that is capable of analyzing the data to maneuver the robotic movement efficiently. This is probably the reason for such slow development in robotic technology. It took years for engineers to make a robot walk. They were struggling to hard code the rules with scanty data. Now with the arrival of AI and affordable IoTs, hard coding is fading away. Robots are evolving noticeably faster. In fact we see new versions of them every year. Very soon we will see a flood of smart, flexible, versatile robots.

AI in Drones

In a captivating TED talk worth watching, Professor Vijay Kumar from the University of Pennsylvania demonstrated tiny drones (flying robots) performing a series of intricate maneuvers, flying through confined spaces without colliding or interfering with each other. These smart robots/drones are capable of aiding in construction, shipping, and even responding to emergencies.

AI in Weather Forecasting

Have you heard of hindcasting? With AI there is no forecasting without hindcasting. Climate models that are currently out there today were first trained with historical data, and the predicted values are compared with actual past events. Historical records that date back thousands of years can help AI developers build predictive models.

Many global companies are keeping aggressive development in these critical areas. The Weather Company, an IBM Business, announced its plans to focus on a project called Deep Thunder that can train machine learning models to predict the impact of weather.

Panasonic is another company that is deep into improving weather technology. It recently purchased AirDat that makes a popular sensor called TAMDAR that can be installed on aircraft. It has started a similar global forecasting system called Panasonic Global 4D which predicted Hurricane Irma more accurately than other models.

Threats to AI

Before wrapping up this chapter, let's look at the technological threats facing AI. There are two broad categories of AI. The first is a hard-coded slave category that mimics only human actions. This category has many names: basic AI, reactive AI, weak AI, or narrow AI (ANI).

The second category is widely called general purpose AI or AGI. This can learn and improve over time, a kind of self-learning. Most AIs that we have today are hybrids with both rigid ANI features and some AGI learning capability.

We shouldn't get too bogged down with these academic terminologies of AI classifications, but there is a strong reason we need to know the distinction. Some AI experts think that it could be dangerous that we still have many rigid ANIs that are not learning from its mistakes. Anyone can hack ANI to knock out our electric grid, damage nuclear power plants, and misdirect robots causing global-scale economic damages.

There is an urgent need to develop smart AIs that we all can depend on. For now we have to be on constant vigil to protect ANIs from outside attacks. We shouldn't get too excited if some utility company adopts an AI. If it's more of a basic ANI with little or no self-learning capability, it could be doing more harm than good as it can't figure out the attackers. It is better that we understand this AI categorization, so we know the threats we are facing.

Most AI software is proprietary, which means we don't know how they are coded. The AI coded by Google may be entirely different from AI coded by Facebook or Amazon. Aptly, open source is beginning to take shape to exchange AI codes and its faster evolution.

Until ANI evolves to a safe zone, there will be a great demand for anti-viruses to thwart ANI hackers. These are the areas of new opportunities. There is also an effort to build a library of ANI talents to quickly evolve ANI. As this library sprouts and the open AI platform widens globally, future opportunities in the AI world would be unprecedented.

Careers in AI

Many AI trend trackers are estimating that more than half the current United States workforce will be at risk in the next decade or so. They are also predicting a plethora of new jobs in AI-related fields.

AI uses many machine learning techniques such as heuristic, deep Q-learning, reinforcement learning, neural networks, and many more coming. Most AI systems are written in Python and R languages, although AI can be coded in any language. In the future as more powerful languages are introduced, programmers would make that shift. If you are serious about learning AI either as a career or just for academic interest, there are many courses available online. Those who are starting new careers and willing to get trained in cutting-edge technologies shouldn't ignore AI.

I hope this chapter gave a glimpse of AI and its current capabilities. In the next chapter we will learn the real threat that is facing us today—global warming.

Chapter 2

Is It Global Warming or Climate Change?

This chapter delineates the global warming's ability to feed on itself. The discussion sets the table for the next chapter, which lays out a detailed plan to fight global warming by exploiting AI's abilities.

The phrase global warming is being slowly rephrased as climate change. But it is too late. The damage has already been done. The phrase global warming is stuck in our minds. Although both phrases are used interchangeably, climate change is more apt for a common person as it relates to the changing weather pattern that we are all experiencing. The phrase global warming became an academic term after it appeared in a 1975 scientific article from Columbia University and since then has evolved into a controversial political term.

Amusingly, during freezing winters many people wonder what the hell happened to the supposed warming effect. So it's not that hard to convince such people that global warming is a hoax. Even talking about a two- or three-degree rise in temperature is equally deceptive for a common person. How can such a small temperature increase possibly destroy our ecosystem? What they don't realize is that's the *average* global temperature and not a local temperature that wavers all day long. We failed to communicate these essential terminologies properly, and our news media is now trying to patch up the miscommunication.

A one-degree rise in average global temperature would be brawny enough to alter the global wind directions. A one-degree increase in average global temperature is burly enough to increase the amount of water vapor above the ocean, causing erratic rain, snow, hurricanes, and snow blizzards. So a little change in average global temperature matters a lot.

Atmospheric research suggests that every one-degree Celsius increase in temperature increases moisture in the atmosphere by more than 7 percent. More moisture means more rain and snow. Disturbed wind patterns mean it would rain unevenly globally. What a catastrophic combination of two mighty forces: higher moisture and disturbed wind patterns. Meaning it could pour heavily in regions that never expected rain and not rain in regions that are dependent on it. With high moisture content in the atmosphere, floods will become very common. The bottom line: with unprecedented floods and droughts we would see catastrophic global economic impact.

According to the National Centers for Environmental Information (NOAA), the average global temperature for January–May 2017 was 0.92 degrees Celsius above the twentieth century average global temperature. The global average temperature is steadily increasing, causing brutal hot and cold conditions.

On the other extreme, people who believe in global warming are convinced they can slow it down with green technology. Green initiatives, green walks, green talks, and green recycling have become our culture. But how much of these green ventures really help?

Most scientists around the world agree that even if humans had not existed, the earth would have warmed anyway but much more slowly. The data from worldbank.org and epa.gov shows that from 1979 to 1982 when CO2 emissions were decreasing (high gas prices led to due to reduced gasoline consumption), there was no change in the rate of increase in atmospheric CO2 concentration proving that even without humans. Obviously it is not the CO2 emission that is of concern, it's the *rapid release* of CO2 into the atmosphere.

Let's look at some surprising facts. carbon dioxide causes only about 20 percent of the greenhouse effect; water vapor accounts for nearly 50 percent and high clouds account for 25 percent. The rest is caused by other greenhouse gases. Even though water vapor contributes the most to global warming, it can quickly condense back into oceans if the temperature drops. However, carbon dioxide remains in the atmosphere for eternity unless washed and absorbed by our ecosystem. If the carbon dioxide level goes down, the atmosphere releases the trapped heat proportionately, condensing the moisture with it. The point is, the amount of water vapor in the atmosphere is decided by the amount of carbon dioxide. Hence the focus is always on carbon dioxide and not water vapor or high clouds even though they together cause 75 percent of the greenhouse effect.

The Intergovernmental Panel on Climate Change (IPCC), the world's foremost collection of climate scientists, is working diligently to bring awareness about global warming to the world. This group produces reports on the current state of the climate system, its environmental and socio-economic impacts, and mitigation strategies that can limit emissions.

Among a long list of future climatic changes predicted by many international organizations including IPCC, I consider three predictions are noteworthy. The first is the size and frequency of hurricanes. These lethal forces have the potential to destroy coastal cities that global economies are dependent on.

The second is the irregularity of rain. Agriculture is still the backbone of many developing countries. In underdeveloped countries, agriculture is their only means of living. With irregular precipitation we will see annihilating effects on human lives and eventually global economies.

The third event is the rise in sea level. Most of our coastal cities are the hub of international shipping on which we all depend. If they are compromised by rising water levels, the economic impact will reverberate throughout the world. We have to pay close attention to these events even if we are non-believers of global warming as it affects everyone's livelihood.

The Carbon Chart[1]

Here is the carbon chart that we all need to know to understand global warming. This kernel chart is essential to compare the carbon reservoirs of the world. All numbers are in gigatons of CO2 (GtCO2):

Underground: 200,000,000

Oceans: 140,400

Fossil fuels: 15,000

Forests: 7,200

Atmosphere: 3,000

Please try to memorize these numbers. These will stay with us for the rest of our lives. As you can see, our atmosphere has the least amount of carbon content. All other carbon sources (carbon sinks) have an inordinate amount of carbon. That means if any of these reservoirs are disturbed, there will be a cataclysmic release of CO2 into the atmosphere. Volcanoes, landslides, earthquakes, and forest fires all disperse a gargantuan amount of CO2 into the atmosphere. There is a constant addition of carbon to the atmosphere all the time.

But in nature these carbon sinks constantly reabsorb carbon too. The problem occurs when the carbon release rate is higher than absorption rate, and that is exactly what we are facing today. We are releasing about 35 gigatons of

---

[1] There are three widely used units: gigaton of CO2 (GtCO2), gigaton of carbon (GtC) and parts per million (PPM). To convert PPM to GtCO2 multiply by 7.8; to convert GtC to GtCO2 multiply by 3.6

CO2 per year by burning fossil fuels and nature absorbs only about half of it.

As you can see from the chart, our fossil fuel reserve still has 15,000 gigatons of CO2 that we can burn before running out. Our atmosphere right now has only 3000 gigatons of CO2. Imagine what would be the impact of burning all the fossil reserve we have. Without any regulation, we would do that very easily and in the very near future.

Land, oceans, and forests have a gigantic capability to absorb carbon. They are natural carbon sinks. While oceans can absorb as much as 30 percent of carbon dioxide, forests can absorb approximately 25 percent. Just these two together they can absorb almost half of the global carbon dioxide that we produce from fossil fuels. The CO2 that we are releasing into the atmosphere by burning fossil fuels would have been easily absorbed by these carbon sinks if we had burned it slowly; they have not been able to cope up with the rapid burning of fossil fuels. If we had burned the same fossil fuels slowly, we wouldn't be discussing global warming today.

This is what we are inflicting on nature. We are producing more carbon than what the earth can absorb, about double the earth's absorption capacity. This is what we call our carbon footprint. If we produce carbon at a rate nature can reabsorb, the carbon footprint is zero. Only when we surpass the amount nature can absorb do we become environmental usurpers.

Global Warming is Feeding on Itself

Land is a huge carbon sink, one of the biggest. Global warming is destroying this great sink. Carbon stored in soil can remain there for thousands of years before being washed into oceans. In just past twenty years, soil respiration released about one hundred gigatons of CO2 into the atmosphere, many times more carbon than humans are now putting into the atmosphere each year by burning fossil fuel. The reasons for such a quick release of carbon into the atmosphere are dried cracked land, landslides, floods, etc. In essence global warming has begun to feed on itself. This truth is hard to swallow. We will find a lot of such grisly realities as we dig further.

Oceans are the second great carbon sinks. Rain washes carbon in our atmosphere and brings it down to the rivers. Rivers feed this carbon to the oceans. The carbon circulates in the oceans for long periods of time before settling at the bottom. Some of it could even return to the surface through thermohaline circulation. Some of this carbon might escape to the atmosphere just like root beer going flat. Any change in oceanic currents could release gigantic amounts of CO2 back into the atmosphere, and that is exactly what is happening now. Adding to this misfortune, when the carbon content increases rapidly, oceans become more acidic and absorb less CO2. Oceans are slowly becoming resistant to CO2. Sadly, global warming is destroying this sink too.

Forests are more mammoth carbon sinks. Forests continuously absorb CO2 through photosynthesis. However, the rain pattern has changed so much in this decade that there are many dried-out forests around the world ready to burn. A university study has shown that forest fires in the contiguous United States and Alaska, release about 290 million tons of carbon dioxide a year. There are forests also getting destroyed by floods. These burned or decayed plants emit their carbon back into the atmosphere. In December 2017 a number of bush fires devastated swaths of Southern California. One, called the Thomas fire, torched 270,000 acres and destroyed more than one thousand homes. Fires in Canada and Siberia have also contributed to huge CO2 emissions.

The good news is that vegetation tends to grow back over the scorched area and will absorb most of the carbon dioxide released. Also, as CO2 in the atmosphere increases, the rate of photosynthesis increases. This is known as the CO2 fertilization effect; in other words, plants can grow well during global warming. However, we have bad news here too. The rain pattern itself is changing, and the burned regions in the world are growing very little vegetation because of scanty rain. Global warming is surely not helping CO2 fertilization either.

Now it's not just coal and oil that are responsible for CO2 emissions; global warming is joining them. Let's put it this way: more ecological destruction means more CO2 flooding back into the atmosphere. The bottom line is even if humans stop adding CO2 to the atmosphere today, global warming will continue to add more CO2 thru its own natural processes of eco destruction.

The Carbon Budget

IPCC has recommended the following carbon budget to motivate fossil burning businesses to switch to solar energy. These are total emissions, not a per year basis.

If we emit 400 gigatons of CO2, there is a 66 percent chance of staying below 1.5 degrees Celsius.

If we emit 1000 gigatons of CO2, there is a 66 percent chance of staying below 2 degrees Celsius.

If we emit a total of 2,400 gigatons of CO2, there is a 66 percent chance of staying below 3 degrees Celsius.

Currently, we are releasing about 35 gigatons of CO2 per year. Which means, in less than twelve years or so, our globe would have blown up its carbon budget and warmed by 1.5 degrees Celsius. If we release more than thirty-five gigatons of CO2 per year—which we might looking at the current global economic growth—we could blow up the carbon budget much earlier.

Then we will quickly reach two and then three degrees Celsius as global warming would become our partner in releasing CO2. If the fossil economy continues to flourish, we will reach 2 degrees Celsius in probably twenty years or so. That is indubitably not part of what we want to pass on to our next generation.

The Warm Hard Truth

Wouldn't it be fascinating to discover that humans are in fact a product of global warming? Without greenhouse gases and without global warming our planet would have frozen to -18°F, supporting perhaps some primitive species.

With that in mind we should look at global warming more as a science than a threat. When we perceive a threat, we invariably try to fight it without paying enough attention to potential aftereffects should we prevail, which is equally dangerous. When we approach global warming as science, we can look beyond the crisis itself.

According to Utah Geological Survey there have been at least five major ice ages in the Earth's history (the Huronian, Cryogenian, Andean-Saharan, Karoo Ice Age, and the Quaternary Ice Age). After each ice age, the planet warms up naturally due to greenhouse gases and again go into cooling phase culminating in another ice age. Even within an ice age are multiple shorter-term periods of warmer temperatures called interglacials. It is these warm periods that give life to complex species including humans.

In this fight against global warming, we should not kill the mother of our own creation, which is the global warming itself. In fact, we need to preserve the warmed planet as is by not allowing it to drift towards extreme global warming or cooling.

Global warming is the most pressing issue for mankind, not for Mother Nature. She'll adapt; we may not. She will survive; we may not. With so little time and so much to accomplish, we don't have many options left. That brings us to the doorstep of AI.

Chapter 3

The Plan to Unleash AI

If you look at the Paris agreement on global warming pragmatically, it has failed miserably. CO2 levels are on the rise, global temperature is still shooting up, and all the ugly effects of global warming are blatantly visible all over the planet. There is political finger-pointing drama being actively played out. There is no discernible defeat of global warming, not a sign. Nonetheless, the people who are involved with this deliberation should be commended for raising global awareness.

When we envision the epic battle against a force as mighty as global warming, the crusade that tops the list is to artificially reduce heat, which would put Earth back to its pre-warming era in terms of global average temperature. But scientists are hesitant to prescribe this geoengineering antidote because of the unknown. While the atmosphere tries to rebalance in this new reality, there could be collateral damages. Scientists fear unintended consequences. The scientific community has failed to understand the impact of global experiments. This is exactly where AI has the potential to decipher the big data of the atmosphere. The upcoming chapter discusses this in detail.

The second stab at global warming is to pull the excessive CO2 out of the atmosphere as it traps the heat. If CO2 is reduced, the heat-trapping capacity of the atmosphere would dwindle, helping cool the planet. We may not need the first strategy of geoengineering if carbon capture is done competently and expeditiously. However, the current global non-AI endeavors are very slow and sluggish. We don't have that much time to waste on political debates either. We need AI to explore ways to reduce CO2 that are inexpensive, accelerated, and adept. I have collected many noteworthy global efforts, all coming up in the following chapters.

The third way and sure silver bullet is to supplant fossil power with AI-driven solar power, the quickest way to peter out carbon release. Replacing our mammoth coal and oil dependency is a gargantuan effort; only AI can find solutions for such a paradigm shift. Here again, I have collected many noteworthy global efforts, all summed up in the following chapters.

Curiously enough, artificial intelligence is a double-edged sword. When we unleash AI on global warming, it will surely fight it better than humans but at a cost. It will take away jobs. This is inevitable; when we architect AI on a massive scale to fight global warming, every industry on the planet will attempt to exploit the smart AI to their own advantage to reduce their costs. AI is already causing job losses in many areas as the technology evolves. However, I found AI has amazing potential to foster the unemployed. This will be discussed in part III of this book.

Those who get caught up in measuring global warming's ability to destroy life as opposed to AI's ability to fight global warming, are missing the opportunity to join this epic battle.

PART II
THE EPIC BATTLE

Chapter 4

The Defiant Global Heat

To reduce global heat scientists around the world are zeroing on one specific approach: brighten the clouds to reflect a partial amount of inbound sunlight back to the space. Changing the earth's albedo, or reflectivity, is what these strategies target. Darker albedos capture heat; lighter albedos reflect heat.

One idea gaining traction is to seed marine clouds with a mist of salt water and other particles including alumina, diamond dust, calcium carbonate, and bismuth tri-iodide, so they reflect more sunlight. This highly controversial strategy is called the *sunlight reflection method* or *solar radiation method* or simply SRM.

What scares scientists about using these geoengineering techniques is that artificially cooling the planet could have unintended consequences. This may cool the planet unevenly and cause side effects such as drought in some places, heavy rainfall elsewhere, and other unforeseen climatic changes.

There is also research being done in stratospheric aerosol geoengineering, where reflective particles are thrown into the upper atmosphere. There are also ideas to position millions of sun shields, mirrors, or discs in space between the earth and the sun in geostationary orbits to reflect heat. These are obviously very expensive and very controversial ventures.

Researchers are also considering using drones to sprinkle fine dust to block sunlight. There are also ideas of using ships to spray droplets of seawater into the atmosphere to form sea-salt aerosols increasing Earth's albedo.

The big question is which country will come forward to implement these unproven strategies? Scientists themselves are skeptical about what could be achieved because there are so many unknowns. The likelihood any of the United Nations' 193 members accepting any of these approaches is minuscule. If no one is willing to ring the albedo bell, why are we wasting our time and energy on traditional research?

What we need are proven, skillfully crafted, affordable strategies, but at the current juncture we don't have sufficient understanding of these technologies. We don't have unlimited time either for long-term humancentric traditional research efforts.

The AI Intervention

When humans come to a technological dead end because of their inherent limitations, it just means that they need help to work beyond their capability. That is the right place for the AI and IoT duo to show their smarter side.

The obvious game plan would be virtual testing: doing the atmospheric experiments virtually with AI software, which can easily accommodate hordes of parameters. The only stringent stipulation for its success is that it needs a mammoth amount of quality IoT data.

The good news is that we need not start from the scratch as for as AI algorithm is concerned; there is already a significant development in this direction. The Green Horizon Project from IBM analyzes environmental data and predicts what-if scenarios.

The National Science Foundation has sponsored a project called the Deep Convective Clouds and Chemistry to measure and analyze storm kinematics, structure, electrical activity, and chemistry to improve our knowledge of how thunderstorms affect the chemical composition of the troposphere.

Microsoft has announced that the company would invest $50 million in the AI for Earth program over the next five years to support the creation of AI that helps reduce climate change and increase crop yields.

When announcing the initiative, Microsoft stated: "We believe artificial intelligence is a game changer," said Smith. "Our approach as a company is focused on democratizing AI so its features and capabilities can be put to use by individuals and organizations around the world to improve real-world outcomes. There are few societal areas where AI can be more impactful than in helping address the urgent work needed to monitor, model, and manage the Earth's natural systems."

As meteorology is intricately linked to chemistry, any rapid research in the field of chemistry would greatly help understand the implications of geoengineering. Here is the current status of AI's capability in the field of chemistry. A team of Australian National University physicists has developed an AI algorithm that created a Bose-Einstein condensate—a hyper-cold gas—which won the researchers Nobel Prizes back in 2001. The experiment involved directing radiation to slow a group of atoms nearly to a standstill, producing the condensate. The AI had the task of monitoring multiple parameters at once and adjusting the process quickly to cool the atoms down. Over dozens of repetitions, it learned how to successfully complete the task.

IBM researchers in Zurich, Switzerland, have developed an AI algorithm that can predict the products of chemical reactions. These researchers have fed the AI with thousands of documented chemical reactions to train on. From the reactant plus the reagents, the AI could guess the most likely end product.

If you look at all these new developments, AI is already being coded to take the challenge and will soon be ready to do some serious lab experiments to evaluate the worthiness of geoengineering strategies. However, the major hurdle is, for AI to accurately predict the outcome of any virtual experiment it needs enormous amounts of data.

Here again we need not start from the scratch. There are more than a thousand weather satellites, both government and privately owned, that collect climatic data. IBM owns several thousand personal weather stations to provide data to its AI system. In addition, every car, truck, traffic lights, even our smartphones could be used to feed real-time data.

Los Angeles is well on its way to become the world's first city to introduce a smart street lighting system, with fully-integrated 4G LTE wireless technology. In a collaboration between Dutch tech and wellbeing firm Philips and Swedish telco Ericsson, the SmartPole project plans to offer LA citizens a combo of wireless technology and a high quality public lighting.

"We are now taking advantage of previously untapped real estate to give our streets better broadband connectivity and future-ready infrastructure, while generating revenue for the city," said LA mayor Eric Garcetti.

Though these data sources appear titanic, as for as AI is concerned, they are insignificant. AI needs data in biblical proportions for accurate prediction of geoengineering strategies. This is where we beckon IoTs.

The good news is the cost of hardware is coming down as is the cost of IoTs, so the dream of having trillions of IoT's around the world may not be so distant. However, the challenge is to rapidly establish more IoTs in the world.

The IoT Enigma

To increase the number of IoTs, one school of thought is to mass produce IoTs and have drones drop them randomly in all remote parts of the world. The IoT sensors have to be redesigned to capture vast varied data from multiple sources. While an intriguing idea, the cost would be astronomical. It is relatively cheaper to spread

IoTs in cities, towns, villages where humans live but very expensive to plant IoTs in remote places. Governments won't do it unless there is political incentive. We have to depend on some philanthropically inclined businesses like Microsoft, IBM, Google, Tesla or other multinational companies who can generously support these kinds of ventures. Even so, we will end up with a limited amount of IoTs. This is a goldmine for the entrepreneurs to come out with a *business model* for private sector investment. There is already an intense competition to produce IoTs. It is just a matter of time they will be all over the globe. IoTs have the potential to become tradable commodities as they produce revenue-generating data, which is the new oil.

AI in Rapid Research

As we are running out of time, rapid research is equally essential to understand our ecosystem. It is not uncommon to see scientists physically going to remote areas to capture specimens and other materials of value for research, a slow and very expensive process. The researchers and their knowledge are highly valuable and risking their lives to collect data or specimen is not worth it. Robots and drones could do this job better.

AI could be trained to manage these machines. Instead of one team of scientists going to one remote area and collecting specimens, imagine an army of thousands of drones and robots all driven by AI going to a thousand different regions to collect data. When AI takes over the management of drones and robots, costs will plummet. You may even see private entrepreneurs joining the race to collect valuable data thru their own drones and selling it back to research organizations. The bottom line, the speed of research matters that is badly needed now.

There is some good news amid the chaos. A bill has been introduced in Congress "to provide for the National Academies to study and report on a research agenda to advance the understanding of albedo modification strategies." The bill is still in committee as of this writing, but its introduction indicates that even the government is serious about albedo modification. The only sad part is that there is no mention of using AI. That could be because of lack of knowledge of AI, for now.

The Missing Piece

If you look at the challenges of global warming in a pragmatic way, very surprisingly everything is in place except data. Look at all the tools we have. We have AI evolving at a decent pace from multiple research organizations and e-commerce companies. We have well-established engineering methodologies to put our strategies into action. The only thing missing is the data for AI to identify which strategies are doable and which ones are not.

We need to produce and plant IoTs at a colossal scale. Unquestionably, the IoT's have to be manufactured with full automation totally managed by AI to bring the cost down. The geographic locations have to be identified with AI competency. The specimen collection for rapid research has to be done with robots and drones maneuvered efficiently with AI proficiency. Inexorably data capture is the weapon we have to ensure our survival.

The Good, Bad, and Ugly of Geoengineering

Geoengineering of any kind is temporary in nature until CO2 is largely reduced from the atmosphere. This is because after heat is removed artificially, it gets collected again as there are sizable greenhouse gases sitting in the atmosphere to trap the heat. Because of this temporary nature, geoengineering has to be done continuously year-round for years or decades until the greenhouse gases are removed substantially. Geoengineering can only buy time and is never a permanent solution by itself. There is also a concern about catastrophic effects like ozone depletion, continued ocean acidification, erratic changes in rainfall patterns, and rapid warming if the geoengineering is abruptly stopped. Hence, geoengineering is the last option left if all the strategies of carbon capture fail.

This takes us to the next chapter that discusses the challenges of carbon capture.

Chapter 5

Capture That Carbon

Carbon capture is one of the most significant steps that the world has taken to reduce the concentration of carbon dioxide in the atmosphere, using both artificial and natural methods. Despite all efforts the carbon dioxide level in the atmosphere is still shooting up. Let's explore how AI could make these carbon capture strategies more efficient, hence affordable and globally scalable.

Carbon Capture and Sequestration (CCS)

Many energy companies around the world are already capturing carbon dioxide on a large scale from their own fossil fuel plants. But capturing carbon dioxide is only a part of the story. Sequestering it underground, called geosequestration, is the most expensive process. Most power plants around the world have been using abandoned oil and gas reservoirs as storage areas. Some companies even drill and store underground. The carbon dioxide is often compressed and transported to these storage areas hundreds of miles away from the source, many times via pipelines. They are required to monitor the gas pressure, and if there is a leak, they have to contain it. However odd it may seem, this is the most economical sequestration method currently available.

Big companies like Shell, Chevron, Exxon Mobil, and NRG Energy have several CCS projects around the world.

Quest, a CCS partnership between Shell, Canada Energy, and Chevron, can capture, transport, and store more than a million tons of carbon dioxide underground annually. Remember we are releasing about thirty-five billion tons of carbon dioxide annually. A mere one million tons of carbon dioxide sequestered appear tiny; however, it is a great achievement for one single project. We need more projects like this.

Chevron, Shell, and Exxon Mobil have a CCS project in Western Australia that can capture three to four million tons of carbon dioxide from natural gas each year and inject it into a deep sandstone formation around 1.5 miles underground.

NRG has a post-combustion CCS project in Texas that can capture about 90 percent of the carbon dioxide from a 240 MW fossil power plant and sequester 1.6 million tons annually.

In Zurich, Switzerland, the company Climeworks is using a unique method called direct air capture (DAC) that captures carbon dioxide directly from the atmosphere. Climeworks's DAC unit consists of stacked shipping containers fitted with small fans that force air through sponge-like filters that soak up carbon dioxide. After a few hours of filter saturation, the box closes, and the collector is heated to 212 degrees F, which releases pure carbon dioxide. This could be stored underground, converted to other products, or sold in the open market to companies that need carbon dioxide to produce products like soda or sparkling water. Though the goal of this capture is to bury the carbon dioxide underground, until the business becomes economically viable, selling carbon dioxide would be the only survival option. Using it in products like soda or sparkling water is obviously not the final goal as it would eventually release carbon dioxide back into the atmosphere.

Climeworks claims it can suck fifty tons of carbon dioxide per year while a tree can consume only fifty kg annually. Although a tree is many times more advantageous for oxygen production and eco-stability, as far as carbon capture is concerned, the DAC needs one thousand times less area compared to planting, and it does not need water or fertilizer. These units can be mounted anywhere in the world.

Failure of Carbon Capture

Despite sequestration's efficiency, the strategy has failed. Unless it's absorbed by the underground soil and rocks, these high-pressure carbon dioxide storage sites have the potential to leak, so they have to be constantly monitored for leakage, and it should be done for the life of the storage site, which is eternity. This adds to the cost of the CCS project and trickles down to the energy bills that we pay.

Furthermore, scientists are skeptical about the durability of these sites against natural disasters like earthquakes and large landslides; more research is needed in that direction. If there is a substantial carbon dioxide leak, not only will all the time and money spent go up in smoke, it will be catastrophic for global warming.

There is a health concern too. There is a concern that the high-pressure gas could leak to the nearby freshwater table. Public fears that carbon dioxide leakage could threaten human lives, and many have railed against some recent carbon dioxide sequestration attempts.

CCS is also a very expensive process. Although governments around the world are forcing the fossil fuel companies to capture carbon, there is no financial gain for businesses to do so except for saving on the carbon tax.

Some companies are capturing carbon from an ethical point view. While others are doing it to reduce their carbon tax, many are doing nothing at all. There are thousands of carbon dioxide guzzling factories throughout the world still active today.

The global transportation sector-which includes cars, trucks, planes, trains, ships, and freight-produces nearly a third of all global emissions. As we can't capture carbon dioxide in individual vehicles, the only option is to convert them into electric vehicles whose impact we are going to discuss in later chapters.

Apart from transportation sector, carbon dioxide could potentially be captured at the source in all industrial units and that effort however is failing because geosequestration approach is not making sense economically. It has financial viability only if we can split carbon dioxide or convert it into useful products that can be traded in the open market. This gives the companies a needed economic boost to scale up their carbon-capturing efforts.

Splitting carbon dioxide also guarantees that the carbon stays on the ground, and there is no need for expensive sequestration and risk leakages from storage sites. However, splitting carbon dioxide is a very expensive process, the good news is that there is a huge demand for carbon around the world.

Look around you; carbon is everywhere, from clothing to furniture to all our household machines. Carbon is the sixth most abundant element on the planet. The carbon businesses will thrive in the future because there is a huge global demand for carbon. The downside is that carbon is being mined from the ground, with graphite and coal as significant sources of carbon. China, India, and Brazil are the largest carbon mining countries in the world and last year respectively mined about 780,000 MT, 170,000 MT, and 95,000 MT.

The very idea of replacing these huge land sources with carbon captured from the air is extremely challenging in part because the potency of carbon is low in the air compared to mined coal or graphite, and the chemical process of splitting carbon dioxide itself is very expensive as carbon dioxide is a very stable molecule. Nonetheless it is very enthralling to know that there are a number of organizations attempting to extract carbon from carbon dioxide including:

Harvard Professor Daniel Nocera has devised a system that uses artificial photosynthesis or artificial leaf or bionic leaf to make liquid fuel from carbon dioxide. In plants photosynthesis does not split carbon dioxide; it only splits water into hydrogen and oxygen. The hydrogen combines with carbon dioxide to generate organic molecules that the plant needs to grow. Carbon dioxide is trapped in the plant and is released only when the plant is burned or decays. That is why we see tons of carbon dioxide added to the atmosphere during forest fires.

Similar research done by the Joint Center for Artificial Photosynthesis funded by the US Department of Energy uses inorganic catalysts to convert hydrogen and carbon dioxide to liquid fuel.

Several companies, including Joule Unlimited and LanzaTech, are working to produce biofuels from carbon dioxide and hydrogen.

Scientists in Switzerland have found a new way to split carbon dioxide using copper catalyst using solar power. The research was funded by Siemens AG and a contribution from Abengoa Research in Spain.

Sandia National Laboratories, in Albuquerque, NM, is working to produce cleaner, more efficient electricity based on supercritical carbon dioxide/Brayton-cycle technology.

Researchers at the University of California have developed a prototype device that can use solar energy to split carbon dioxide into oxygen and carbon monoxide

(CO), an important industrial chemical, which is normally produced from natural gas.

Other research at the University of California is attempting to split carbon dioxide with an ultraviolet laser.

CO2 Solutions claim to have developed a technology that uses a natural enzyme called carbonic anhydrase, which exists in all living organisms., as a catalyst to absorb carbon in power plants.

Global Thermostat's proprietary technology uses low-cost, leftover heat to capture carbon from power plants. The company claims the technology can absorb more carbon if more heat is produced.

In all the above examples, be it splitting of carbon dioxide or conversion of carbon dioxide into useful, tradable product, the influence of AI is minuscule. AI is not being harnessed to make these endeavors more efficient and cost-effective. There is no unified effort to make AI a central focal point to fight global warming. Many of these efforts are still manual-labor-centric approaches. This is the reason why carbon capture is still expensive and not globally scalable. AI intervention is exactly what we need to face these challenges.

AI Intervention

Chemistry is the backbone of all the above experimental ventures. The good news is that AI is making inroads into the field of chemistry. Many companies are already developing AI to read the periodic table along with data on past experiments to predict chemical reactions. Here are a few of the pioneers.

Zymergen in California is using AI to do lab experiments. While robots do the physical experiments, AI does the data analysis. The AI is open-ended in the sense that it is not hard-coded to do any specific task; instead, it does random experiments by manipulating various parameters and analyze the data using the knowledge of basic sciences to produce a database of immense value.

The California startup, Transcriptic, is already building robots that can conduct experiments. This will free researchers from manual drudgery. The experimental data once stored digitally is easier to mine and analyze. This will ultimately lead to cheaper and more reproducible science.

While the research community is focusing on splitting or converting carbon dioxide into useful, tradeable product, AI is simultaneously evolving to enhance chemistry. These two fields are complementary to each other and assuredly we will see some commercial projects soon. Until then the traditional CCS efforts must go on however inefficient, risky, and expensive they are.

The solace is that there are a number of equally robust natural processes that can absorb carbon dioxide. Below is a brief survey of some of those amazing discoveries.

Natural Sequestration

A research project in Iceland has shown that by simply pumping carbon dioxide underground in certain regions, it can react with calcium, magnesium, and iron to form carbonate minerals like limestone. This could lock carbon dioxide for a long time, and we need not have to worry about carbon dioxide leakage.

In the mountains of Oman, researchers from Columbia University have found that much of the country's landscape contains peridotite, a special rock consisting of olivine and pyroxene that absorbs carbon dioxide and makes it part of the rock. They are trying to find out how the earth's minerals have the capability to mop up the excess carbon dioxide. If AI can learn this natural chemical reaction, we could recapture the excess carbon dioxide in the atmosphere fairly economically.

AI can sniff through global data and determine what parts of the world have similarly exposed peridotite. This is where data capture using IoTs, drones, and robots become relevant. The idea of sending drones and robots to remote parts of the globe and spreading IoTs around the world that we previously discussed begins to look more propitious in the light of carbon capture. It all boils down to how economically we can capture the big data of our ecosystem and how dexterously AI could analyze this mountain of information helping us in rediscovery.

AI in Reforestation

Here is an earthly way of capturing carbon. Plants absorb carbon dioxide from the atmosphere through photosynthesis, which is why forests are great, and the more of them, the better. But when forests burn or decay, carbon dioxide is released back into the atmosphere. Global deforestation contributes to more than 10 percent of total greenhouse gas emissions. Reforestation is undoubtedly a great way to capture carbon naturally.

A former NASA engineer has launched a new startup called BioCarbon Engineering that would use drones to plant one billion trees a year. The process involves what is called precision planting, where drones track tree planting potential or restoration potential, and if the region is good for planting, the drones will shoot germinated seeds into the soil at a speed of about ten seeds per minute, which would add up about one billion trees per year. This is an amazing effort in the right direction.

The success of such projects depends on how precisely they calculate the restoration potential to prevent wasted time and money. AI could help ensure more precise evaluation of restoration potential by scanning through a multitude of data such as historical precipitation levels, plant species, how tall they grow, their carbon dioxide absorption capacity, local geology, and site history to determine the best places for forests to thrive. It would be very prudent to work alongside AI; otherwise, the life of forests will be very brief, and all efforts will be in vain.

The great news is that global efforts both by governments and individual volunteers have resulted in substantial carbon absorption close to one gigaton of carbon dioxide per year. However, much more progress could be made if AI is adapted in all these efforts. A word of caution for the volunteers who are involved in developing forests: ill-planned planting could become a victim of drought, a worthwhile reason to work alongside AI.

More Geoengineering

Many global researchers are making headway in developing natural techniques to make our ecosystem absorb more carbon dioxide. For example, ocean fertilization adds nutrients like iron, urea, and phosphorus to the ocean in selected locations to increase marine food production, so the seawater can absorb more carbon dioxide from the atmosphere.

Ocean alkalinity enhancement is where rocks such as limestone, silicate, or calcium hydroxide are powdered and dissolved in the ocean to reduce acidity and boost its dexterity to store carbon.

Enhanced weathering exposes large quantities of minerals that will react with carbon dioxide in the atmosphere to produce compounds that can be stored.

Even though all these mega strategies look very promising, we have hit a roadblock; who is going to pay for large-scale implementation? It could cost trillions of dollars to implement them globally because we always estimate the cost of a project with manual-labor in mind, be it in research or implementation. No surprise then that many research findings never see the light of the day. However, all these shortcomings could be eliminated if we adopt drones and robots enhanced with AI's competencies. Here are a few global endeavors rapidly moving in that direction.

Liquid Robotics, a subsidiary of Boeing and in collaboration with NOAA is striving hard to protect the Hawaiian marine sanctuaries. The wave glider, an autonomous surface ocean robot, is being developed to monitor the area and gather a wide spectrum of data including pH and salinity levels in the water. Such efforts would be highly expensive with manual efforts. We need more of such ventures.

Stanford University has developed a humanoid robot called Ocean One that has thrusters to navigate and two arms and stereoscopic vision to explore ocean depths to collect data for research that would be hard and expensive with human involvement.

Students at MIT have put their AI software to work on underwater vehicles to the test in the Charles River and are creating robots that can go places where humans simply can't collect data.

If you look at all the above methods of reducing carbon, whether natural or artificial, carbon capture is tied to data capture, so AI can sniff through the big data and guide the robots and drones accordingly. It emphasizes that there is an immense need for swift eco-data collection using IoTs.

AI-enhanced drones and robots would be of immense value in both efficiency and low cost and human-labor force don't stand a chance in these endeavors. It is not just nutrient dispersion these machines would also collect valuable data for AI to skim through.

AI can't fight global warming by itself. It is ultimately the engineering processes that fight global warming. AI is just an algorithm, but it has an immense capability to improve efficiencies of the engineering processes thereby making them affordable. This is how AI fits into this blood game.

The green initiatives only buy us some breathing room and won't fight global warming. Even great innovative technologies might not make a dent if they are not adopting AI to become financially feasible. We have to turn the fight against global warming into economically viable investments. Only then will such efforts bear fruit.

Government Intervention

It is worthwhile to know how governments around the world are spurring their economies to contain global warming. Apart from a carbon tax to encourage carbon capture, a new concept called carbon trade—or cap-and-trade—has been implemented in many countries. It's a market designed to trade carbon emission allowances to encourage companies to limit their carbon dioxide emissions.

In the EU a cap is set on carbon dioxide emissions and permits are given to companies to release a certain amount of carbon dioxide per year. If they exceed their allowance, then they must purchase additional permits to cover the excess release. However, if they stay below the cap, they can trade their unused allowances.

The carbon tax and carbon trade are opposite sides of the same coin. A carbon tax sets a price for carbon dioxide emission. More emissions create more taxes, leading to higher cost. It's hard to sell expensive power. More taxes slow down the economy, so governments have to tweak the carbon tax, so it won't become a burden on the economy.

On the other hand, carbon trade caps the number of emissions and lets the market determine the price. Here again the cap has to be adjusted to have maximum benefit and minimum impact on the economy. Although both have their own pros and cons, it is ultimately the governments that decide which is the best for their economies.

Though the intent of carbon tax and carbon trade is to incentivize companies to peter out fossil fuel and switch to solar technology for faster emissions reduction, how fast these businesses embrace AI and recognize it as the ultimate weapon to fight global warming will decide our fate.

Switch and Capture

Merely imposing carbon regulations and hoping that the switch will somehow happen only satisfies some political motives.

Even though the goals of the carbon tax and carbon trade are well-intended, they have remained a weak force to initiate the switch to green energy because of the expensive manual-labor centric engineering processes.

Remember; even after we stop burning fossil fuel by switching to solar completely, we still need to pursue carbon capture, as there is a well over 3000 Gt of CO2 sitting in the atmosphere. We need to bring this below to at least 2000 Gt of CO2, a pre-Industrial Revolution level.

Currently we are releasing about 35 GtCO2 every year to the atmosphere. We need to stop producing and start absorbing carbon dioxide. We need to absorb at least 100 Gt of CO2 annually so that we can reduce 1000 Gt of CO2 in ten years. More optimistically we could absorb at least 50 Gt of CO2 annually, so we can reach that limit in twenty years' time.

If you look at these astronomical numbers, we have a lot of work to do in a short span of time. So infusing AI into every carbon capture strategy make sense. We shouldn't let this opportunity pass by. Now the burning question is can AI trigger rapid growth of renewable energy? The next chapter is all about building amazing solar power plants driven by AI.

Chapter 6

Soliciting the Solar

Solar energy comes to Earth in the form of sunlight. All plants on earth store this energy through photosynthesis. Herbivorous animals get this energy by eating plants and in turn are eaten by carnivorous animals. Except for some rare species that derive energy from chemical reactions, all life on Earth derives energy either directly or indirectly from the sun.

So why didn't we invest in this abundant energy source in the beginning instead of digging for fossil fuel?

The answer lies in our technological evolution. Our very first engine was a steam-powered engine, not a solar-powered engine. During that time, our knowledge of utilizing solar energy was primitive at best. The world celebrated the invention of the first steam engine because it was the greatest evolutionary product of that time. We embraced the technology and our economy began building on this energy source almost immediately. Capitalizing on this technology, we were able to move many more goods quickly, evolving at a steady rate. Gradually, coal power became the backbone of our economy.

We ate solar food but traveled on coal!

Then we started using oil, a more sophisticated source, for almost all of our energy needs. In spite of its sophistication, it has not totally replaced coal even today.

Coal is so deeply-rooted in our economy that according to the Centers for Disease Control, there are still more than a thousand active coal mines around the world feeding hundreds of thermal power plants.

The energy generation from both coal and oil is very well-established, and both are quite vast resources. However, they have one serious drawback: neither source support a sudden surge in energy demand. This is how initially alternative sources of energy like solar, wind, hydro, geothermal, and tidal came into existence. The sad part is not much investment went to research and development of renewables and they are still not able to compete with fossil fuels.

Coal and crude oil have ruled the world for a long time. We have dug, burrowed, and mined the planet to our heart's content. The impact is nothing short of catastrophic. It's not only global warming we're concerned about but <u>unsurmountable</u> dependency on these unsustainable energy sources. Another factor of great concern is the participation of developing and underdeveloped countries that are consuming considerable energy, especially oil and coal.

As the global economy expanded, demand for energy increased and the energy industry was unable to meet the demand quickly enough. It takes years to build thermal power plants and refineries. The sudden increase in demand and insufficient supply caused energy costs to rise. We have hit many energy-inflicted recessions in the past.

Back when we first struck oil, we knew oil would one day be depleted. Still we celebrated and built mega industries around this non-sustainable source. This tells us that entrepreneurs may or may not take us on the right path; they are there to compete and succeed in business. It is the responsibility of governments to create level playing field and guide economic growth in the right direction. This is where all governments around the world failed. The sun has so much energy that merely capturing an infinitely small fraction of it would make us energy sufficient. Tapping into such a mega source is the wisest decision we could ever make.

Solar Success Story

Amid all the challenges, solar energy is finally becoming very competitive with fossil fuel as the price of photovoltaic modules has dropped by almost 40 percent in recent years, and the efficiency of solar cells is steadily increasing. Solar panels now account for only about a third of the cost of a power plant. To cut costs further and finally win the race with fossil fuels, an obvious solution was to put solar-robots, or solbots, to work.

California-based Alison Energy is using robots to install solar farms and substantially reducing labor costs by as much as 75 percent, making it competitive in a fossil fuel world. To reduce costs, the company is using extruded concrete instead of steel to build rails. It uses robots to ride the concrete rail and clean the dust on solar modules. Also in California, SunPower is using drones to survey potential sites for a solar power farm that can fit the most solar panels to lower costs.

NEXTracker designs and builds advanced single-axis solar trackers that can intelligently track the sun and produce more power—even during cloudy days—compared to other standard tracking systems, a great boost to the solar industry.

Unquestionably, technologically advanced machines have made a towering impact in the solar industry by saving tons of money. If we can boost electricity production by 5 or 10 percent at a solar plant, that's a game changer in terms of economics. With solar intensely competing with fossil fuels, every second of solar exposure counts, and any attempt to improve solar cell efficiency has a big role to play in that industry.

That Is Not Enough

All the above technological developments, however advanced they seem, are not tenacious enough to replace fossil fuel. Let's look at the reality of solar industry. The total global installed capacity of thermal (coal) power is currently about 4000 GW. On top of that, every year the thermal (coal) energy demand is increasing by at almost 120 GW. But over the past 10 years our solar industry globally has grown on average only about 50 GW per year although for last 2 years, with all the technological advancements, increased to 100 GW per year, which means it has barely satisfied the additional growth of energy demand and is not making a dent on the existing coal power industry. The process of replacing coal with solar has not even started.

Here is a quick glimpse at the current major solar power plants around the world.

2.2 GW Bhadla, India
2.0 GW Pavagada, India
1.5 GW Tengger, China.
1.0 GW Datong China.
0.8 GW Longyangxia Dam, China
0.9 GW Kurnool Ultra, India
0.6 GW Kamuthi project, India
0.6 GW Rancho Cielo USA.
0.5 GW Topaz in USA.
0.3 GW Noor Complex, Morocco

And there are many other smaller projects being built around the world totaling globally about 500GW. Compare this to mighty 4000GW of coal installations.

The world is celebrating the arrival of electric cars with the grand hope that someday they may replace gasoline as fuel. But the sad truth is most electric cars are charged at home using the traditional electric supply, which primarily comes from coal, oil, and natural gas. That means we have merely shifted the problem from cars to power plants. Instead of burning fossil fuel in the car, we are now burning the same in power plants.

Imagine the load on the power grid if all one billion vehicles with combustible engines in the world switched over to electric cars; it's estimated the additional electricity surge would reach at least 2000 GW. A total of whopping 6000 GW (4000GW from coal + 2000GW from vehicles) would be needed to meet this power frenzy.

Obviously we will start digging for more coal or natural gas to meet this demand unless solar power generation grows very rapidly. Conversion of gasoline cars to electric cars is just the beginning of another saga of energy replenishment.

To replace this mammoth 6000 GW of coal power in 10 years or so, we need to jack up solar growth to at least 600 GW per year from the current 100 GW per year. We need to move at a rapid pace. There is tremendous pressure on renewables, especially solar, to meet this unprecedented demand to avoid burning more fossil fuels. It simply means that to replace coal and oil, the growth in the solar industry has to be spectacular, such as an innovative, AI-based approach that has the potential to grow exponentially.

The Silver Bullet

The science of mass-production teaches us that it is possible to produce enormous amount of solar energy in the quickest possible time with a technique called replication. Replication is the process of producing multiple replicas of solar power plants at the same time. AI-driven robots and drones can easily bring about replication, which is exactly what we need in the energy industry today.

It's possible to program AI to manage robots and drones in assembling solar panels, transporting the panels to a power plant site, assembling a solar power plant, and then to hook up the plant to the smart grid. We are pushing AI's capability toward a fully autonomous solar-plant building industry, which can sustain itself and be replicated around the world.

Once programmed these robots will perform tirelessly until the power plant assembly is complete. Initially the cost will be high, as skilled labor is needed to plan, build, and program the AI and wire it to the robots. We might even need substantial energy from fossil fuels to build such a plant. After the completion of the first plant, the army of robots used for that will be able to replicate additional solar energy power plants in other designated locations by themselves.

There will be no further need to start the process from scratch or enlist human talent to design or redesign new blueprints or drawings. In fact, no skill transfer will be needed, period. All the information fed into the robots during the first power plant would be reused for subsequent plants, except perhaps for some information about the topography of the new sites that can be easily learned by the AI system. A solar business can be fully automated with this approach.

Imagine competing businesses that could replicate such an army of robots continuously. Within a short time we could end up with thousands of solar power plants all built and managed by AI. The current fossil fuel dependent businesses would inevitably switch over to solar. Most Arabian countries that are rich in fossil fuels are rich in the desert sun too. All they need to do is just to switch from one technology to the other, and they have already started that process, with experts estimating many oil rich countries will run out of their current oil reserves by 2040 at the latest.

As the technology behind solar cells becomes even more sophisticated with AI-aided research and as AI builds better, bigger power plants at a much lower cost, solar energy will be highly affordable. It will be the cheapest we have ever paid for such a bountiful, renewable energy supply. If AI is fully exploited to build a massive solar industry within decades, like ants building their colonies or bees building honeycombs, without any human intervention solar plants will proliferate all over the globe.

Let's deep dive to envision how cheap energy could create abundance. Cost of energy heavily influences the cost of all products. Cost of any product essentially depends on three resources—energy, raw-material and labor. When energy becomes cheap, the mining cost which primarily depends on energy will plummet. With cheap energy and low-cost raw materials the products will be very affordable. This invariably puts pressure on labor and eventually the low-skilled manual labor will be callously replaced by AI-driven versatile robots, making the products cheapest ever.

Consumers will be buying as never before as the prices are low. With sky high demand, industries will be producing products to their fullest capacity. With AI-driven machines, manufacturing will be smart and scalable, driving further innovation.

Today the patenting, prototyping, manufacturing, marketing, and warehousing that comes with bringing a new product to market is a high-risk investment. Because of these risks, many inventions from ordinary folks never saw the light of the day. They just died with the inventors. But cheap energy, smart manufacturing and virtual research through AI will engender a new breed of innovators bringing many great products and services to market.

Product affordability increases the standard of living immensely. With an inordinate level of abundance, the societal responsibility of supporting the unemployed who have lost their jobs to the AI, will not be a burden.

Easier Said Than Done

The grand vision of architecting solar plants autonomously is a Herculean task. Let's look at the realities of such a dream. The upfront costs are very high as are the financial risks. A typical industrial robot with the latest application-specific bells and whistles costs between US$80,000 and US$100,000. To program these robots, wire them up to an AI brain, and then train the AI to maneuver these machines and configure the whole system to autonomously build the solar power plant needs a massive team of programmers, engineers, and technicians to make it happen. It is truly a paradigm shift in the world of automation both in terms of planning and implementation.

The most difficult task in this endeavor is estimating the risks involved while treading unknown territory followed by securing financing for a highest-priced, experimental initiative such as building a fleet of automated machines to build solar complexes. Certainly it will be dependent on private investors, not governments, and even then, who will be willing to step forward?

To make such a plan economically feasible, I believe there is only one answer: off-the-shelf, intelligent robotic systems that are prebuilt, prewired to AI, and preprogrammed with cognitive ability would change the landscape of any industry. When prebuilt intelligent systems become available in the market, they will become darlings of the manufacturing industry. The AI would easily learn the existing manual systems and seamlessly replace human labor and work fully autonomously. Such projects are also easy to estimate with measurable risks that attract financial investors.

The great news is, global manufacturing is moving towards such a digital revolution, called Industry 4.0. Industry 4.0 is commonly referred to as the fourth industrial revolution. As you will recall from history textbooks in grade school, the first industrial revolution was driven by steam power. The second industrial revolution was all about mass production using assembly lines and the third industrial revolution was molded by Internet and information technology. The fourth industrial revolution is being heavily influenced by digital manufacturing. This includes "smart" systems including robotics, the Internet of things, cloud computing, and cognitive computing.

The goal of Industry 4.0 is not to fight global warming—yet. The driving force for the emergence of such a digital movement in manufacturing is severe competition, which has led to collapsing profit margins. The current generation of skilled workers is retiring, and it's difficult to find people with matching skill sets to replace them. New products, new ideas, and new technologies are constantly hitting the market, making the skill-hiring process even more difficult. Latest technologies like driverless vehicles, augmented reality, virtual reality, and IoTs are growing faster with big data, machine learning, and mobile computing. All these new technologies are forcing the manufacturing industry to move towards robotization and digitization to survive the competition.

In the current solar power industry most onsite assembly projects are still manual as smart, versatile multitasking robots are not there yet. This is what we need in the solar industry. This is what Industry 4.0 is desperately trying to build.

Event organizers around the world realize that Industry 4.0 is becoming mainstream and there are multiple Industry 4.0 conferences and symposiums for many specialties happening every year around the world.

How fast Industry 4.0 brings intelligent systems to the marketplace will decide the pace of automation in the solar industry. The pace will be much faster if global think tanks can draw a distinctive relationship between Industry 4.0 and global warming, so there will be a conscious effort to speed up this process. Colleges and universities will have an equally responsible role to sync up their existing curriculum, however advanced they are, with the latest cutting edge technologies as and when they come out of the research rooms into the market, so the college grads will bolster the skilled Industry 4.0 workforce.

Fossil Fuel Mess to Solar Mess

Although the world is desperate to replace fossil fuels, whether solar energy is the right substitute for the fast-growing economy of the future is worth exploring. Solar energy is surely green energy; however, the impact of green energy on the economy may not be green. The energy source itself may not be harmful to the ecosystem, but its consequences could be. Here is a quick glimpse into noxious pitfalls we might encounter as the world attempts to replace fossil fuels with solar.

It is estimated that when the entire fossil industry is replaced by solar power, globally the land used for solar power plants will catapult to about 120,000 square km (46,332 square miles), nearly half the size of Arizona. Obviously, the solar power plants are not concentrated in one place but are distributed throughout the world, but the challenge is solar power generation is not efficient during winter. For example in Germany the installed solar power is about 30 GW. News reports state that it has captured about 50 percent of the national power supply. That is true—but only in summer. In winter it only generates about 10 percent of its capacity. So in such places the solar power plants have to be ten times bigger to make up for the winter shortage. Consequently the large scale land usage will have environmental impact. That problem could be offset to some extent by having wind turbines built in conjunction with the solar farms to also generate power during winter. That reduces the size of land to some degree but of course depends on the average wind speed in those regions.

Installing a wind turbine is less complicated than solar panels because the entire wind turbine can be mass produced in a factory using robots and autonomously transported and installed in high-wind zones. However, wind-powered energy generation is not as steady as solar powered energy; wind speed fluctuates by season and even by time of day. Obviously these wind and solar power plants need excess capacity to supply power adequately in winter. That means the land area that is estimated above would shoot up at least five-fold in cold climates. Those numbers would be much higher if there wasn't sufficient wind energy.

The other challenge is that oversized wind-solar power plants apparently produce surplus energy in summer that may not be needed, causing some shifts in the economy. If power becomes much cheaper in the summer, industries might start producing more goods during summer and less during winter. Then entire industries will start building around energy availability. Additionally, as battery technology improves, people will buy batteries and store cheap energy during summer and use it in winter. This economic shift poses new challenges to the power plant industry in terms of financing, risk estimation, and the environmental impact of battery waste. We will see many such unique non-green impacts on the economy as we move more away from fossil fuels and toward solar and wind energy.

The greatest non-green impact of cheap energy comes from the exponential production of goods. With cheap energy the world will consume goods like never before. The production of goods will be exponential and so will the raw-material demand. Underground mining will be rampant to satisfy the hungry market and to build solar plants and wind turbines. Not only will substantial land be appropriated by these power plants, but the earth will also be increasingly mined and burrowed unscrupulously year after year. If the economy grows by say 5 percent each year, so will the land sizes of solar and wind power plants. We'll be moving from a fossil fuel mess to a solar mess.

This potential calamity must force us to develop innovative technologies to produce energy that is truly green: carbon-free, radiation-free, and compact. Here is a quick peek at the latest global endeavors that are already working to find that true green energy.

Commonwealth Fusion Systems, a private company, in collaboration with MIT is attempting to produce clean, abundant energy via fusion technology. Using a new class of high-temperature superconductors and ultra-powerful magnets, they are able to regulate fusion reaction to smash hydrogen atoms together giving off helium and huge amounts of energy without nuclear waste.

Similarly, scientists in France are attempting to generate power with fusion technology. The International Thermonuclear Experimental Reactor (ITER), a massive tokamak fusion reactor, is under construction in France with an investment of $14 billion dollars from countries like United States, Russia, China, India, Japan, and South Korea. The scientists are hoping to generate power by 2025.

The US Department of Energy's (DOE) Princeton Plasma Physics Laboratory (PPPL) is also involved in studying tokamak experiments.

Scientists in the UK are also working on nuclear fusion. Atkins is partnering with Tokamak Energy to generate the first electricity by 2025.

Fusion holds the most promising clean and renewable energy worldwide. It has no radioactive waste and is a great alternative to the land grabbing wind and solar power plants.

However, we should be cautious about cheap, abundant energy and not chop the branch we're standing on. Generating cheap energy and creating abundance in society may lead to destroying our planet as we mine it to our hearts' content to satisfy the accompanying exponential industrial growth. The potential environmental impact of mining is mind-boggling. Underground mining causes soil erosion, development of unstable land with sinkholes, earthquakes, loss of biodiversity, groundwater contamination by chemicals leading to health problems for nearby residents, and so on.

These catastrophic consequences of cheap, abundant energy must spur us to look at deep space voyages to mine on asteroid belt instead of on Earth.

Here is a quick glimpse into the world of asteroids. An asteroid belt is a region of space between the orbits of Mars and Jupiter where millions of asteroids orbit the Sun. The asteroid belt contains millions of asteroids and they come in a variety of sizes from as small as less than a mile across to as large as one-quarter the size of our moon. Some metallic asteroids contain rich mixture of gold, platinum, nickel, magnesium, iridium, palladium, and other precious metals such as rhodium, osmium, and ruthenium.

The main challenge of asteroid mining is the distance. Mining will be extremely expensive with today's technology and hence not many have paid much attention to this futuristic option. However, as we move into fusion era and autonomous robotic world, asteroid mining—and space exploration in general—are researched in greater detail.

At some point in the future, as we empower ourselves with true green alternatives like fusion energy we should plan on winding up the solar mess that we have created here on earth. We must conceptualize our dexterity to protect the planet and keep it safe.

Solar power is only a stepping stone to go beyond fossil fuels; it's not the end game. It will ultimately be atomic energy sources like fusion reactors that take us to the next era of technological evolution.

Although the future looks bright, for now we should focus on coming out of the current fossil fuel mess we have concocted. Robotics, drones, AI, and many other cutting-edge technologies are all coming up at the right opportune time. Industry 4.0 is giving the world a big hand in developing smart systems. We should build solar and wind power plants as much and as fast as we can until we replace fossil fuels entirely.

I hope this discussion makes us contemplate beyond global warming. We need to protect the planet not just from global warming but from unconscionable mining that is bound to happen as a consequence of cheap energy.

Chapter 7

The Face of Victory

We have explored enough strategies so far to fight global warming. Now let's step back and think rationally about what's really going to work for us. We currently have three options on the table: a geoengineering strategy to reduce global heat, a carbon capture strategy to reduce CO_2, and a solar strategy to move away from fossil fuels. Which of them provides workable solution to global warming? At what stage can we say that we have defeated global warming? What does the victory really look like?

The ultimate goal of this blood game is to rollback our ecosystem to the pre-fossil fuel era to reclaim the stable climatic conditions mankind has flourished in for millennia. The spotlight ought to be on a switch-to-solar and capture-the-carbon strategy. For this strategy to work in our favor, we must switch to solar from fossil fuel sources at every available opportunity and relentlessly capture CO_2 until the earth can naturally release the trapped heat. That will also save the world from the unintended consequences of geoengineering.

But the inspired global community expeditiously capturing CO_2 may overdo it. Unless they know exactly where to stop, they may overdo it and unintentionally push the planet toward global cooling. Our ecosystem could also absorb more CO_2 than expected as a result of efficient global reforestation and de-acidification of the oceans, adding to inadvertent cooling, which would disturb the climate just as much as rapid global warming does and require our intervention to pump some CO2 back into the atmosphere to keep it warm. The point is, we must closely monitor CO2 levels even after we pull the planet out of the current global warming crisis, a truly Herculean task of maintaining an eco-balance. If we can master the art of keeping our planet's ecosystem in equilibrium, not allowing it to warm up or cool down, then we can claim to have won the battle against global warming. However, this victory is not a one-time event; it's a perpetual process. If we falter, the earth will again drift towards a warming or cooling phase, putting climatic conditions out of balance.

Both global warming and cooling are natural processes, meaning we need to hold our ecosystem hostage in artificial balance, which may have obvious ill effect on the planet's ecosystem and all life on it. When we should let our planet go free from human clutches is another debate after we learn from balancing it.

For now our focused intent should be building proficient AI, capturing high-quality data, and eventually pulling our planet out of a global warming phase. To achieve this we need time, of which there isn't much. That magnifies the immense value of green initiatives that help us reduce our carbon footprint and slow the current pace of global warming. Green living may not be the cure for global warming, but it can buy us some time to plan and execute more effective strategies.

If we are not able to switch to solar in a decade or so, then we'll have no other option but to use geoengineering strategies despite their dangers. Such a situation would be an admission that AI hasn't worked either in carbon capture or in solar strategy. And if AI has not worked in those two strategies, then AI is probably not going to work in geoengineering either. It's not the AI algorithm being challenged; it's the lack of data. It would mean we had failed to capture quality data for AI to function to its fullest potential.

I am not pessimistic by any stretch; in the same breath I am not blindly optimistic either. If we succeed in completely switching to solar but fail to capture sizable carbon in time because of our inability to act fast, at least the cheap energy would drive enormous growth in robots, drones, and smart machines to protect humans. When a warming planet shows its ugly face through raging hurricanes, ferocious forest fires, and violent floods our robust machines would be capable of building new cities spontaneously in safe places with little or no effect to our economy.

If climate-change driven extreme weather makes the planet surface uninhabitable for humans, our smart machines could build life enclaves resembling self-contained metropolises. If the situation further deteriorates, our smart machines could build underwater worlds without affecting our technological evolution or the economy. That is where there is tremendous value in green technologies, which would enable this transition to happen smoothly. When we move away from our current eco-dependent life to enclosed biospheres, our technologies have to be one hundred percent green; emissions have no place in those cocoons. In those protected environments the only technologies that would flourish are green technologies. Going green now and preparing for such eventualities is an incredible opportunity we can't afford to ignore.

Even in those artificial enclosures, we would continue to pursue our carbon capture strategies to make our planet habitable once again. Humans won't give up easily. Our fight against global warming will never stop until we win. All that is possible only if we can survive the current onslaught of global warming and switch to solar in time.

Successfully switching to solar only means that we have made it, and it is only possible with AI proficiency. AI-managed solar is a win-win proposition. It is the ultimate silver bullet that has the potential to change our global destiny. That is unfailingly a momentous gift to our next generation.

That is the true face of victory.

Part III
Collateral Damage

Chapter 8

Men Not at Work

It is estimated that more than four million taxi and truck drivers will lose their jobs if autonomous cars become ubiquitous. That technology is just around the corner. The world is set to embrace it without giving a second thought about the consequences of this technology. Or should they? For the majority of the population, self-driving is a big relief. It is assuredly much cheaper to board an autonomous taxi than a taxi with a driver. It's a no-brainer to imagine most driving jobs would be under threat.

With online sales going thru the roof, the retail apocalypse has finally descended upon the United States. Isn't it more comfortable to order online than going into crowded stores? With a few mouse clicks, your product will be at your doorstep in a couple of days, and even that could change to few hours in the near future with Amazon's plans to utilize drones, automated vehicles, and robots, all managed with efficient logistics. Many retail brick-and-mortar stores are already closing down as they can't compete with e-commerce. Brace for this: there were more than fifteen million people working in the retail industry as of 2018. Not all jobs will go away, but most will.

It is also expected that almost ten million jobs will disappear in the construction industry if 3-D printed homes hit the market. China is already building livable homes using

3-D printers. A printer can build a five-hundred-square-feet house in twenty-four hours for less than $10,000, which would normally cost $50,000 or more if manually built. This is the price tag before the mass production of 3-D printers. As the market blossoms the price will further plummet. A few networked printers could print a large, luxury home in one day. A $1 million home could be built for 20 percent or less. Three-D technology is all set to destroy the traditional construction industry.

Manufacturing, agricultural, tourism, hotels, restaurant, transportation—pretty much every industry will soon be affected by technology. What a mess we are going to witness.

When we nurture AI to fight global warming, undoubtedly it will threaten our jobs. Now the challenge is not just to combat climate change but to survive the collateral damage. It is an ugly fight indeed.

Advanced technologies are infamously called disruptive technologies. That's what their nature is. They disrupt traditional technologies, traditional businesses, traditional careers, shaking the status quo. Disruptive technologies are not meant to destroy jobs. They are meant to improve our standard of living. Job loss is inevitable collateral damage. Disruptive technologies emphatically create new jobs, new careers, and a whole new world.

Twenty years ago few imagined that Google would one day be a multinational company. Today the company has well over sixty thousand employees globally. Companies like Amazon, Apple, Microsoft, and Facebook have created millions of jobs globally directly or indirectly. People realized the demand for high-tech jobs, got trained, acquired skills, and became the backbone of these companies, building new careers. It's been a massive transformation in the job market. Universities too have evolved new curriculums. Much of this has happened over the past two decades. Now recently AI's rapid growth has people worried whether they have enough time to jack up their skillsets to go back to work.

What about those who get left behind in the job market, the modern-day versions of blacksmiths and horse-carriage drivers? The word that comes to our mind is humanitarianism. The truth is we could feed the unemployed only if we have abundance. If we build an opulent society then yes, the basic needs of human beings—housing, transportation, food, and healthcare—can be provided. The nation can take care of the unemployed and the poor if there is abundance in at least these four areas. There are already social movements demanding some sort of basic income for the poor and unemployed. Global Think Tank is actively deliberating a universal basic income (UBI) for those left behind. No matter how much we debate, this can only be achieved if there is abundance. With the current high cost of living, the UBI is impractical. Any technological development that increases the costs of these basic necessities is a disaster for UBI. And that is exactly what is happening today.

Could we exploit AI to foster these four critical areas? After having gone through multiple examples on the capabilities of AI, it is not that hard to imagine the possibility of harnessing AI to influence these four critical areas to increase our economic abundance. The next four chapters address the pros and cons of this approach because like every advanced technology that came before it, AI is a double-edged sword.

Chapter 9

Print a Roof Overhead

Will the world's next megacity splash out of a 3-D printer? Imagine printing a city with the click of a mouse. That is where the 3-D printing technology is heading. The Dubai-based company Cazza is currently planning to build the world's first 3-D-printed skyscraper in Dubai by 2023. It is committed to supporting the emirate's vision to 3-D-print 25 percent of all of its buildings by 2030.

What is a 3-D printer anyway? Imagine your printer has very thick ink, and you print the same image over and over on the same piece of paper. The ink would accumulate to give a three-dimensional appearance. The commercial 3-D printers utilize materials such as polymer plastic, wood fiber, cement, or metal filament, depending on the need.

The 3-D printers are an advanced version of your home printer. Three-D printing, also called additive manufacturing, is the process of making three-dimensional solid objects from a digital file using additive processes, where an object is created by laying down successive layers of material until the entire object is created. Each of these layers can be seen as a thinly sliced horizontal cross-section of the eventual object. It starts with making a virtual design of the object that is to be created. This virtual design is made using a computer-aided design (CAD) software or using a 3-D scanner to copy an existing object. A 3-D scanner builds a 3-D model of the object to be printed.

Initially 3-D printers came on the market to create prototypes or samples of proposed items before venturing into expensive mass production. As the technology evolved, many manufacturers especially car companies used 3-D printers to create parts for assembly, particularly certain expensive parts. Now 3-D printers are used in all large manufacturing industries to produce many critical parts reducing the need for inventory and transportation.

After years of talk and development, 3-D printing technology is finally entering the construction industry. China is currently a leading driver of 3-D printed houses and seeing more around the world is looking increasingly promising.

There are many potential benefits. Every year in the United States, four hundred thousand workers are seriously injured or killed doing construction work, according to the Occupational Safety and Health Administration (OSHA). Construction also invariably generates tons of waste including wood, drywall, and roofing materials that are sent to the landfills. And construction contributes significantly to environmentally harmful emissions. Automating the construction process using technologies like 3-D printing saves lives, reduces costs, and is better for the environment.

Cazza is not the only company disrupting the construction industry. The San Francisco-based startup, Apis Cor, built a four-hundred-square-feet house in a

Russian town within twenty-four hours for a mere $10,000. The company used a mobile 3-D printer with a nozzle to squeeze out concrete. Then workers manually painted it and installed the roof, wiring, hydro-acoustic, and thermal insulation.

A house is an assembly of individual finished products. However, the main structure is the most expensive to create. That is where 3-D printers are winning. Once the structure is complete, how we finish it varies. We can do away with simple materials or indulge in exotic interiors.

The Dutch firm MX3-D is going in a different route. It is using a combination of metal inert gas welders and robotic arms to print large metal structures faster and cheaper. China-based Winsun has built fully functional office space in Dubai. In California, Massachusetts Institute of Technology students have attempted to build a livable house using earthy green materials.

The materials used in 3-D printing vary. In Madrid, Spain, Acciona and D-Shape collaborated to build a pedestrian bridge using micro-reinforced concrete material. In the Philippines, the owner of Manila's Lewis Grand Hotel has 3-D printed an extension using sand and volcanic ash. In Massa Lombarda, Italy, the firm Wasp has built a complete village with 3-D printers, using mud, clay, and plant fibers.

The Italian firm D-shape has built a 1,110 square meter house in Amsterdam that looks like an infinite loop. It could be used for exhibition space. Another company has built a bicycle bridge in Gemert, Netherlands, that features eight individual, reinforced, and pre-stressed concrete pieces assembled together. Yet another company has built a canal house in Amsterdam that is made up of thirteen unique rooms.

The list is growing by the day. In the last five years, 3-D startups have sprung up all over the world. There is a huge entrepreneurial opportunity to grab a piece of this global enterprise. It is worthwhile to watch YouTube channels to see how these 3-D houses are built worldwide.

AI Intervention

Using 3-D printing in construction has created some unease regarding safety. In traditional human-built homes, builders make sure the structure is safe by employing various proven engineering methods. Humans have perfected this technology over many centuries. Now with 3-D printing, that human element is replaced by machines. This is a paradigm shift from traditional construction. Similar to self-driving car technology that is going thru sensor anxiety, the 3-D printed houses are facing structure anxiety.

In 3-D printing, the major challenge is that a small defect in a critical location of the building could lead to a catastrophic collapse of the building. As 3-D printing does not follow the traditional pillar and column architecture, this newly found technology could work well for smaller buildings. However, when it is scaled up to large structures, it faces technological challenges along with fiscal justification. This is what has slowed down the development and implementation of this technology. Now with the arrival of AI, there seems to be a huge jump in achieving that needed safety in buildings.

Remember AI is not a construction technology. It's a software that is immensely capable of processing big data and self-learning. AI makes 3-D buildings much safer by scanning for imperfections in real-time during construction itself. Especially if IoTs are embedded in critical locations of the building, they can provide valuable data in real time. They can measure compressive forces, tensile forces, structural strain, stress distribution, and if any minuscule changes occur it instantly transmit its analysis to the cloud. AI can continue to monitor the stability of the structure with data from IoT's after construction ends, making such buildings more secure than traditionally built structures. Moreover, if the building in question totters, AI learns from its mistake.

Once AI is embraced by the construction business, it will start disrupting the current business model by eliminating the need for human engineers and laborers. AI can efficiently maneuver the construction robots and can enhance the nozzle performance by determining the right size and shape, depending on the material used. AI can do this instantly if quality data is fed.

AI can easily boost the speed of construction by deploying robots in the right places and navigating them skillfully. The robot maneuvering needs a huge amount of data that only AI can handle. If humans are assigned to this task, they will take ages hard-coding each robotic movement.

With chemistry and metallurgical big data, AI could even suggest viable alternative materials for the structure to suit the topography. Basically AI becomes the 3-D printers' brain in construction.

There are many 3-D printing companies already using AI technology, such as the London-based startup Daghan Cam Limited. It is retrofitting an industrial robot with 3-D printing guns and rewiring it to AI, so the machine can see its own structure while building and learn from its mistakes. The result was one of the largest models in a single piece. The Bartlett School of Architecture is now backing this work to use in more commercial projects. Another British company, AI Build, is also using AI to speed up 3-D construction.

Traditionally, when structural engineers evaluate the strength of buildings, they use approximate calculations. However, with embedded IoTs AI could get more accurate structural stability information in real-time. The data will help AI to learn to become a better builder. As a consequence of AI's influence, 3-D printing would arguably be the most disruptive technology ever to shake the trillion-dollar global construction industry.

Today a three-bedroom, three-bathroom house averages around US$300,000. Consider how the real estate market might shift if we incorporate 3-D technology and the same house can be built for US$60,000 or less. Lower-income families would breathe a sigh of relief while the rich could afford more houses. Both scenarios would mean a significant increase in housing demand, creating a significant number of jobs. Of course, most of the jobs will be high-tech jobs.

It's not just the 3-D construction industry that will experience this mega growth. Supporting industries such as 3-D printer design, 3-D printer manufacturing, 3-D printer marketing, 3-D printer R&D, 3-D printer retail part selling etc., will enjoy cascading growth. Consequently, AI would threaten a large number of unskilled jobs in those industries as well. But the sheer volume of construction made possible by 3-D technology would absorb many of the job losses for a while at least. Then as automation continues to grow, unskilled workers will find it harder to hang in there. This category of unemployed workers will badly need UBI, which as we previously noted would not be practical until house prices are affordable. As the world moves toward low-cost 3-D printed homes, even the poor and unemployed can easily afford comfortable homes with their share of UBI.

Just to bring costs into perspective, in August 2005 Hurricane Katrina resulted in $105 billion in damage with 1,836 total fatalities. If the cities and towns had been built using 3-D technology, the loss would have been significantly lower.

As of this writing the hurricane Florence has hit Carolinas devastating both human lives and the local economies. Imagine building 3-D houses for those displaced people. Better yet, imagine building 3-D homes and moving the people to those homes well before such hurricanes hit the coast, totally eliminating human casualties and ill effects on the economy.

In the United States nearly 34 percent of an average worker's income goes toward housing. For the poor the percentage is higher. The general population will embrace 3-D-constructed housing because their mortgage burden would substantially lower. If you look at it pragmatically, the positive impact of 3-D printing on the economy will outweigh its negative impact of job losses. Governments around the world should consider offering subsidies, tax writeoffs and other incentives for 3-D printed houses, especially in hurricane areas, where global warming is creating ever more powerful storms.

The bottom line is we can't ignore AI as global warming encroaches on us and our homes.

Chapter 10

Reinventing Transportation

When I booked my first Tesla Model 3, I was only two hours late, and my booking number was 150,000! No car maker in the history of automobile manufacturing had ever sold that many cars online so quickly—and before the company even had a site to assemble it. After that shock the entire auto industry woke up from hibernation and started scrambling to switch over to electric car technology just to survive the competition.

With all the car makers producing electric cars, imagine what the impact will be on the industries that are dependent on gasoline cars as more people switch to electric vehicles. A whole lot of businesses would fold. Gas stations would obviously be one of the front liners. There are more than half a million gas stations in the United States alone. Out of those only a few would survive as charging stations. The rest don't stand a chance.

The next shockwave yet to come is self-driving or autonomous technology. In this book I use the words *self-driving* and *autonomous* interchangeably, both meaning *driverless*. Interestingly, these terminologies have different meanings in other parts of the world. In India for instance, *self-driving* refers to a regular car without a hired driver, meaning you have to drive your rental car by yourself and no driver will be provided! For non-Indians that definition might seem odd, but traditionally in India, rentals used to always come with a driver. Only recently have car rental companies in the country started offering driverless—as in chauffer-less—cars. So please be aware of the regional slangs.

Although Tesla, Google, and Uber appear to be in the forefront of the game, pretty much every car manufacturer has invested heavily in this technology, and we will soon see countless numbers of self-driving electric cars on the market. Although autonomous technology could fit into any car type be it electric or gasoline, most autonomous cars on the market today are electric. For these obvious reasons, in this book autonomous refers to self-driving electric car technology.

Here is what autonomous transport technology can offer us. It could prevent hundreds of thousands of traffic crashes, save millions of gallons of fuel, and free up time for countless numbers of commuters. Reduction in traffic accidents means saving billions of dollars in healthcare costs. Decades ago there were fewer vehicles and fewer accidents. According to the National Highway Traffic Safety Administration (NHTSA), US motor vehicle crashes per year cost over $1 trillion in loss of productivity and loss of life.

As most self-driving cars on the market today are electric, reduction in gasoline usage means better health with clean air. Some cities in the world are almost uninhabitable because of the smog caused by gasoline usage pollution. Environmentalists claim that breathing in Delhi, India is equivalent to smoking forty cigarettes a day.

What's Slowing Down the Self-Driving Car Industry?

Self-driving technology is all set to hit the road. What slowing down its arrival are the legalities. Legal experts are still figuring out how to deal with accidents caused by this new technology. In today's world, the legal processes and procedures are pretty much in place for human drivers. As it stands, drivers are currently legally accountable for accidents in traditional cars. But with self-driven cars, there are other considerations. The car owner, the car manufacturer, and the software provider invariably get into the legal tussle. Many legal complications have to be ironed out. Until then self-driving will just be an add-on feature turned on at the driver's risk. All Tesla drivers have to keep touching the steering wheel every few minutes to keep the automated system going. This is a precaution to make sure that driver is awake while in auto-mode. That is the stage we are in now. Technology is ready, but not the regulations.

Safety in Autonomous Cars

In self-driving cars, if you look at it pragmatically, safety is all about data. Most car crashes happen because of a lack of data. We blame software for accidents, but in reality it is the real-time data that saves lives.

Take the example of the 2016 Tesla crash that occurred in Florida. The autopilot sensors on the Model S failed to distinguish a white tractor-trailer crossing the highway against a bright sky. This is an automated system that is fully dependent on data for safety. If you want to blame someone, it's the missing data!

The accident could have been easily avoided in multiple ways if you examine it from a data perspective. First off, if the system had topological data coming from satellites, like real-time Google Earth, it would have figured out that there was a tractor-trailer crossing the highway. The second possibility would be if the tractor-trailer itself were transmitting data—the way airplane transponders do—that in turn was captured, then the crash could have been averted.

The other possibility would be if any other automated vehicle saw the tractor-trailer crossing the highway and had that data been shared, then the crash could have been averted. In the near future, as more vehicles become automated, there will be more data on the roads and every vehicle will know every other vehicle on that road and these kinds of dumb accidents won't happen.

The other exciting thing is that in the autonomous world even the satellites would be receiving and throwing back immense amounts of data for safety. While such data would be invaluable as far as safety is concerned, in the same breath it's overwhelming too. This is where AI would become inevitable to decipher this towering bigdata and direct the autonomous systems to work safely.

It is not hard to imagine that in the future AI would collect the big data coming from all sources and would figure out not just a tractor-trailer passing in front, but in fact it could even predict the position of all the vehicles for miles ahead via the flood of real-time data.

If you look more closely, in the future data becomes an integral part of our safety system. This means our future vehicles will be filled with the Internet of things (IoT) in all critical parts sending real-time data, so AI would process it and maneuver it safely. That means no surprise brake failures or engine outages. Every crucial component will be sending data via IoTs, and AI would know the exact safety level of the vehicle. If the vehicle is not safe enough, the vehicle won't even start.

For automated vehicles *data is the eye, data is the brain; if data is missing it is blind.* In the future we expect that as data grows exponentially, safety concerns will fade out.

Future of Self-Driving Technology

One of biggest industries that would be negatively impacted in the future is automotive parts and repair. In self-driving cars the sensors need to be in flawless condition all the time. If a mechanic makes a mistake, it could cost human lives. The mechanics of the future will be under greater stress, and the job demands a higher technical skill level. For every accident, owners will have to prove that they themselves did not tamper with the system and that all maintenance and repairs were done by certified mechanics.

This will take us to a new world of sensor-anxiety. In today's manually-driven cars even if the engine breaks down, at least you have control of the vehicle. But in driverless cars, you are at the mercy of those sensors. Sensor anxiety might be so worrisome that it raises the question: is car ownership really worth it. Then how about just summoning a self-driving cab when you need one? With an autonomous taxi, you not only stop worrying about the sensor, but you also don't have to deal with any car maintenance period. For car rental companies, it's economically feasible to maintain a large fleet of cabs and monitor them constantly to make sure all sensors are in good shape.

At some point in the future, human drivers will become a rarity, and gasoline cars will be relegated to vintage clubs. With all gasoline cars outdated, gas stations shutting down, and car ownership a rarity, the automobile industry will move into the next era of digital transport fully managed by artificial intelligence (AI).

Here is how the future of commute could look like. On a typical day, you get up in the morning, get ready to go to work and summon a cab. When you board the car, the AI in the car uses its facial recognition technology to know who you are, where your office is, and even what credit card to charge. All you need to say is: *Go to the office,* and it will either take you to the office if it is nearby, or it will take you to the nearest train/bus station if the journey is too long or not suitable for car commute.

You board the train/bus, and when the destination is reached, you come out of the train/bus, and another cab will be waiting to pick you up. Here again, the cab knows who you are and where your office is. You don't have to be anxious about the route it takes or the number of trains/buses it suggests or anything of that sort. You just follow the directions from the cab, and it will take you to your destination in the shortest possible time depending on the traffic situation on that day. You can totally focus on tasks of value during transport without being distracted. Same comfy ride coming back home. What a hassle-free commute! It certainly bolsters the productivity at workplaces.

In that example the entire commute is dependent upon data: the data of routes, data on traffic conditions, data of train/buses schedules, and so on. AI will put all this together and save you plenty of time. Once we get into these kinds of AI grand comforts, there will be no turning back. The economy would get a big boost as employees become much more productive by leaving the hassle of commute to AI.

There could still be few people who wish to own and drive cars for fun. People could even continue to drive gasoline cars, as long as gasoline continues to be sold. Insurance companies will charge them exuberant premiums as they are risky human ventures amid digital transportation. When all gas stations are completely rolled down, it will ultimately make the ownership of gasoline cars obsolete.

The idea of digital transport is uncanny. Every cab on the street knows who is sitting in them and the cars would exchange information so swiftly that the entire fleet of cars in a city could be easily tracked. It might feel like an invasion of privacy, but that is what we chose! Loss of privacy is not happening by accident; we let it happen intentionally in the name of ease and comfort. There is no turning back.

Talking about privacy, regular folks who commute to work every day need not be uptight. In fact, that would give them a legit alibi to prove they have a normal life. Anything strange should certainly be accounted for. This helps keep the communities safe.

The Job Threat

As the world makes its transition from car ownership to car usership, we could see many companies flaunting their fleet of self-driving cars for the public to rent and roll. It could be rental car companies like Hertz and Alamo or taxi companies like Uber and Lyft that get into this lucrative car rental business.

When so many companies begin to compete on the road, consumer expectation will change profusely. They expect the autonomous car to be stylish, clean, and luxurious with all the latest features; otherwise they will just dismiss it and summon another. Clunkers don't stand a chance. That will tremendously impact the volume of car manufacturing. In order to maintain new cars on the road, the competing companies will have to recycle the cars frequently. In today's world, we keep our cars on average between five and ten years. In the automated future, you may not see cars that are older than a few months, which means the number of cars manufactured could increase by almost one thousand-fold! Consequently, car manufacturing facilities will begin to pop up like mushrooms all over the country, leading to massive employment and entrepreneurial opportunities. However, most of these will be assembled by robots, likely meaning that the employment opportunities will cater to the technologically skilled. Although some unskilled workers could be rehired, many may not make it.

The other major job creator in the car industry indeed would be car detailing. With customer expectations hitting the roof, it would be expedient for the cars to be impeccably detailed after each use. This competitive market will flare up many jobs, careers, and entrepreneurial opportunities—but again, all whirling around high technology. The car detailers of the future will not be cleaning cars with hands but with robots. Humans will be remotely monitoring thousands of such stations. Yes, jobs are plentiful but highly skilled.

Here Comes the Hyperloop

The world is craving for high-speed transport. Today our global transportation is moving at snail speed. Ships take almost a month to cross oceans. Even the fastest international passenger airlines can take more than a day to fly half-way across the globe. We are paying a huge price for this sluggish travel in terms of slow economic growth. For elderly people global travel is a nightmare.

The reason behind sluggish transportation is fuel efficiency. Shipping companies save fuel costs by traveling at an optimal speed of 20 knots (23 mph). Anything more, ship safety will be compromised, and at the same time more fuel will be used. This is a ridiculous speed, however on the sea it's the best we get.

The same reasoning goes with airlines too. Airlines go at speeds for optimal fuel use. Recommended cruising speeds for commercial airliners today range between about 480 and 510 knots. Going faster eats more fuel per passenger-mile. As of today, 600 mph is the limit we could reach. This speed is plentiful compared to land travel; however, for long distances it looks darn slow.

For any global economy that acutely depends on shipping, a month of ship travel from one end of the globe to the other can only be described as deplorable. All the economic parameters like cost of inventory, delivery time, even the marketability of a product, profoundly depend on speed. Even though the cost of transportation initially seems higher using higher speeds, the reduction in inventory and high volume delivery would balance it out. Economies would grow more rapidly with speed. Global economies, especially in the advanced world, are craving for

high-speed transportation. Why is our transportation so
slow?

Let's talk about the culprits of stunted transportation.
When it comes to air travel, wind friction is the cause for
limited speed. At sea, water resistance is the speed breaker.
For high-speed trains it's air drag. When it comes to road
transport, it's the human at the wheel that puts the break on
speed for safety.

When we put all this together, the two things that
stand out in preventing high speed are drag and safety. The
obvious approach that comes to mind is an enclosed
transport where air can be sucked out, reducing the drag,
and at the same time with safety IoT restraints, the AI-
maneuvered vehicles can go safely at high speeds. The only
limitation to the speed would then be the sophistication of
the technology. Let's look at some of the global efforts in
pursuit of high-speed transport.

Elon Musk (Tesla, SpaceX) first publicly announced
his idea of a hyperloop in 2012 that would use reduced-
pressure tubes in which passenger pods ride on air bearings.
His concept of the Hyperloop Alpha was first published in
August 2013. SpaceX has built an operational hyperloop
test system at its headquarters in Hawthorne, California. It's
approximately one mile long with a six-foot outer diameter.
To encourage innovation SpaceX announced the
Hyperloop Pod Competition to challenge college student
teams to build the best transport pod. In the first
competition, held in January 2017, below are the winners:

Overall Score: Delft Hyperloop (Delft University of Technology, Netherlands)

Fastest Pod Award: WARR Hyperloop (Technical University of Munich, Germany)

Safety and Reliability: MIT Hyperloop (MIT, USA)

Pod Innovation Award: Badgerloop (University of Wisconsin, USA) and rLoop (Reddit)

Best Performance in Operations: UMDloop (University of Maryland, USA)

In the August 2017 competition, the first prize went to WARR Hyperloop. In the July 2018 competition, WARR Hyperloop pod hits 284 mph to win SpaceX competition.

The hyperloop concept was open-sourced by SpaceX so people across the globe could take the idea and further develop it. SpaceX also provides services to innovators and universities across the world interested in high-speed transportation technology and solutions.

Since then many companies have been formed and are working to advance the technology. The company Hyperloop One has proposed a business case for a three-hundred-mile hyperloop route between Helsinki and Stockholm that would tunnel under the Baltic Sea and take less than thirty minutes. Hyperloop One is also doing a feasibility study for hyperloop routes between Dubai and greater United Arab Emirates. It is studying a cargo hyperloop to connect Hunchun in China to Russia's Far East.

In May 2016 Hyperloop One kicked off a global challenge for comprehensive proposals of potential hyperloop networks around the world and selected proposals for the following ten routes: Toronto/Montreal, Cheyenne/Denver/Pueblo, Miami/Orlando, Dallas/Laredo/Houston, Chicago/Columbus/Pittsburgh, Mexico City/Guadalajara, Edinburgh/London, Glasgow/Liverpool, Bengaluru/Chennai, and Mumbai/Pune.

Hyperloop One was rebranded as Virgin Hyperloop One after a substantial investment from the Virgin Group led by Richard Branson. Virgin Hyperloop One has also built a fully operational test site in Nevada.

Another company, Hyperloop Transportation Technologies (HTT) USA, is doing preliminary studies to link Bratislava, Vienna, and Budapest. It is doing similar explorations to connect Bratislava, Brno, and Prague.

It looks like India is a strong market for hyperloops as well. Many companies are competing here too. HTT has proposed a hyperloop route between Chennai and Bengaluru, taking a half-hour. HTT is also proposing to link Amaravathi to Vijayawada with a six-minute ride. Virgin Hyperloop One has proposed a route between Pune and Mumbai, beginning with an operational demonstration track. Indore-based DGWHyperloop is proposing a hyperloop between Mumbai and Delhi.

AI to Make Hyperloop Cheaper

One of the roadblocks in the evolution of hyperloop technology is the expensive infrastructure. Tunneling is one of the biggest costs. Today's hyperloop technologies are depending on huge tunneling machines worth millions of dollars. These are not only expensive to manufacture, but they are also very pricey to transport and install at the site. Even the operation of such tunnel drilling machines requires an inordinate amount of energy. If the machine breaks down for any reason, the project comes to a screeching halt until it is repaired and put back to work. The entire drilling task depends on this expensive machine. This problem could be fairly easily resolved with AI. Instead of one large drilling machine, we could replace it with millions of ant-like robots. Ant locomotion could be the future of robotic tunneling systems. It might surprise you that there are already endeavors in this direction.

Research conducted by the Georgia Institute of Technology's School of Physics studied fire ants in laboratory settings. Using video and X-ray computed tomography, researchers have uncovered fundamentals of ant locomotion in digging tunnels that future robotics could use. This was sponsored by the National Science Foundation. Similar studies were done at the New Jersey Institute of Technology as well.

The robot ant tunneling technique, if it becomes a reality, could burrow holes like ants do instead of one huge expensive drilling rig. Each of these bugs would carry its own batteries that could get frequently charged. We could easily mass produce millions of these little bugs and use the army of little drillers to build the tunnel economically. If programmed well, the entire army of ants could be fully controlled by AI, making it completely autonomous. If one ant fails, it will not be a show-stopper. These bot ants would also evolve as AI learns from them.

There are already commercial ventures in Europe in this direction. Badger is a consortium consisting of seven partners from five different European countries. Its goal is to design and develop a small, worm-like, autonomous underground robotic system that would drill, map, and navigate underground space. It uses a conventional rotary cutting head with an ultrasonic drill, which pulverizes rock with high-frequency sound waves. The soil will then be sent to the surface. It moves forward like a worm. The rear part of this worm will clamp itself to the wall. As it moves it will reinforce the tunnel behind it using a 3-D printer.

In the future with these less expensive, easily mass-producible, self-learning, self-evolving mini bots all steered by AI, we won't need expensive tunneling machines anymore.

Hyperloop Safety with AI

In this super-high-speed transport, data is life and death. We need data from every corner of the transport system. This should remind us of the sensory organs of AI: the IoTs. The hyperloop needs millions of IoTs embedded in every critical system like propulsion system, transmission system, suspension system, braking system, electric system, and so on. We also need IoTs on the tunnel structure of the hyperloop to get data on structural stability. We need IoTs pretty much on every critical component to monitor the system for safety and stability. The more data, the better.

What do you think would handle this immense amount of big data getting collected from all IoTs? AI's capability to make decisions becomes indispensable. AI can look at the mounds of data and prognosticate if anything would compromise safety. As AI gets real-time data, there are no surprise part failures. All the future failures would have been predicted and taken care of well before the journey starts. Any unexpected outside forces like earthquakes or bomb explosions are sensed in real-time and would bring the system to a halt.

AI can even suggest alternative ways to improve the hyperloop technology to augment both speed and safety. For example, it may do analytics on big data and suggest alternate aerodynamic shapes of the pods traveling inside the loop or economical propulsion system to increase fuel efficiency or alternate suspension system to increase safety and so on. In the future, if all the hyperloop systems around the world talk to each other, AI would learn quickly and offer us better safety. Think of AI as an efficient designer, builder, and operator, all in one. Hyperloop can't ignore AI in its evolution.

Now imagine the impact of cheap transport on the economy. Both autonomous driving and hyperloop transport would boost economic growth. High-speed and low-cost transportation affects the cost of everything we buy. With AI-induced abundance, even the poor and unemployed can easily afford basic lives with their share of UBI. Looks like we are becoming more comfortable now talking about UBI as housing and transportation would become affordable to the poor in the new era of AI.

Chapter 11

Inventively Serving Food

Wouldn't it be enthralling to order food in our own kitchens just like we do in restaurants, with chef-quality food arriving promptly at our table? That's where the food industry is heading now. UK-based Moley Robotics has developed The Moley Robotic Kitchen, which the company says "is revolutionary for more than its automated cooking; it is also an iTunes-style library with a growing collection of recipes from around the world. Initially it starts with a plate of ingredients. Eventually the system will be accessed anywhere remotely, with a delicious meal awaiting your arrival home."

After placing separate containers of measured, washed, and cut ingredients on designated spots and pressing the start button, the Moley will download the recipe from the Internet and cook. It will even clean up after itself.

The food industry is a highly labor-intensive sector, and the price is largely related to manual labor costs. Harvesting, transportation, warehousing, and even food preparation are the services that add cost to food. AI is establishing itself in this complex food industry, which could have a phenomenal effect in terms of reducing the cost. Let's look at some of these labor intensive industries and explore how AI is impacting those sectors.

The company Harvest Robotics has developed a strawberry picking machine that can serve eight acres in one day, doing work equivalent to thirty workers. Harvesting machines are not new to the agriculture industry. However, the latest AI-driven machines use object recognition software to identify multiple types of fruits. They are very efficient as they self-learn and learn from other machines. As there are worker shortages in many parts of California and Florida, these machines are keeping the industry going.

Blue River Technology, owned by John Deere, has developed a robotic weed killer that can identify the weeds using AI and spray herbicides with high precision, reducing the cost of weed control. The AI needs a large amount of varied data including varieties of weeds so that the machine can learn to differentiate between a plant and a weed. This kind of AI-assisted weed control can save almost $40 billion annually on weed control, a huge game changer in agriculture.

Although chemical weed killers seem revolutionary, they have their own chemical foot print. They also give rise to herbicide-resistant superweeds which are part of today's reality. Chemicals are highly harmful to our eco system, although they seem to do wonders in short term. Fortunately many alternative technologies are on the way. U.S. Department of Agriculture is experimenting with sandblasting weeds. The Norwegian University is experimenting on killing weeds with laser. All these technologies would greatly challenge the agrochemical companies that are dominating today's market. Days are not far away for crawling, climbing, buzzing micro-robots or weedBots that can bite-off the weeds instead of killing them with chemicals. These weedBots if maneuvered by AI, will be highly economical and ecofriendly. Few weedBots could easily manage an acre of plantation. They can also be designed like mini flying bots programmed to protect the plants from pests, insects and other crop destroyers again avoiding pesticides. They can even look after the health of the plants by sampling their tissue-data and advice the plantation owners about the maintenance needed to increase the yield. They can also upload their local data to the Internet-cloud making the big data much more valuable. By looking at global data, businesses can compare and contrast the significance of weed and pest killing with and without chemicals. Possibilities are endless if AI is harnessed well.

SkySquirrel has developed an AI technology that uses drones to take aerial pictures of vineyards. It compares the photos of grape leaves to its database to detcct diseases, pests, and poor plants. This saves tons of money in manual labor required for maintenance.

Sorting fruits and vegetables is yet another labor-intensive task that employs about two million people. Tomra Systems uses AI in its fruit and vegetable sorters, which uses technologies like infra-red spectroscopy.

The Japanese company Kewpie is using Google's TensorFlow machine learning software to quickly inspect ingredients that go into food products. With AI, these companies can achieve good results at substantially reduced costs.

Let's explore the world of food preparation which a highly labor intensive industry. Here is a unique way of capturing popular recipes. Coca-Cola has devised a unique way to learn user preferences. It has installed self-service soft drink fountains in numerous restaurants, where customers can mix and match and create their own flavored drinks. This data was fed to AI to figure out what the majority of customers want and came up with a new flavor. AI recommended Cherry Sprite to be a favored combination, and Coke eventually launched the product. In the coming years we will see more of such AI generated recipes in the food industry.

Researchers at the University of Nottingham in the UK in conjunction with the company Martec of Whitwell have come up with an AI technology that uses ultrasonic sensing and optical fluorescence imaging technologies to improve how food processing equipment is cleaned. This reduces water use, energy, and time, saving millions of dollars.

In China nearly two hundred restaurants are using AI technology from KanKan to detect if employees are wearing masks and head covers to help meet the health regulations.

Looking at all these developments, AI is pretty much everywhere from seeding to harvesting to cooking food. AI is going to have a massive impact on the food industry as it has the potential to bring down costs.

Impending Job Losses

In the food industry most of the jobs are done by unskilled manual laborers, so job losses will become rampant as AI takes over. But one unique thing with the food industry is that the number of farms, the number of food trucks, the number of grocery shops, and the number of restaurants are all limited by population size. Meaning the population of a city decides the number of workers needed in its food industry. Meaning, the food industry may not absorb all the unskilled workers who lose their jobs as a consequence of AI.

The good news is that while AI eliminates human jobs, it has the potential to feed the unemployed and the poor. A worker who gets paid $10 an hour picking strawberries earns $80 a day working eight hours. For a family of four, that's barely enough for food and housing let alone healthcare and other expenses. This is the reality many unskilled laborers are living today.

With AI, food could become much cheaper, enabling governments to afford subsidizing food for the poor and unemployed. The food stamps that cost the government billions of dollars will suddenly become less burdensome. When we resolutely consider implementing UBI, the only hurdle is the expensive healthcare.

Chapter 12

Intelligent Care of Health

This chapter discusses two burning topics in healthcare: AI's ability to deflate skyrocketing healthcare costs and the impending job losses in healthcare stemming from AI takeover.

Amid dissensions, economic pundits agree on one thing: technology is driving our rising healthcare costs. Isn't it a bit outlandish? The same technology that made the laptops, mobile phones, and other gadgets smarter, made them cheaper too. Why on earth would technology make healthcare expensive?

The difference is consumer electronics are products, while healthcare is a service. The laptops and mobile phones are mass-produced and exported worldwide, bringing down their cost. Global competition has made these products low-cost. Sadly, healthcare is a highly doctor subservient and hospital-reliant service that is hard to globalize—for now.

Just to illustrate this dependency, say a patient goes to a hospital with a kidney stone. With the current technology, the stone can be fragmented and removed in a simple outpatient procedure. However, to get to that point is a long journey. In most cases patients arrive at an emergency room with severe abdominal pain. They get checked up by physicians, who order some lab tests or scans, and then the patient is moved to the procedure room. When all is said and done, the patient has utilized expensive resources including physicians, nurses, technicians, etc. This is how the cost escalates even if the actual treatment is simple. This kind of service reliance is not there in electronic gadgets.

If the laptop or mobile phone manufacturers invest billions of dollars in bringing out the next great feature, the cost is easily absorbed when millions of customers worldwide purchase the device. That is not the case with healthcare, where if there is a new invention, it can't be sold directly to the patients. It has to be approved by the Federal Drug Administration, adopted by the hospitals, protocols have to be set, and all the healthcare professionals have to be trained to use it.

There is a huge service dependency that makes it cost sensitive. Every time a new medical procedure comes out to the healthcare market, there is a high probability it would increase the cost of healthcare. The cost of healthcare could be attenuated by minimizing these resource dependencies.

AI to Reduce Dependency

Healthcare costs can be substantially reduced if the current healthcare procedures are made more efficient with AI capability. Here is an example. The average cost of a colonoscopy in the United States is over $3,000 and takes about an hour for the procedure. Believe it or not, the success rate of detecting benign polyps is not 100 percent. It means that a doctor could possibly miss cancerous polyps during a colonoscopy, resulting in expensive procedures later on adding to the healthcare cost. Remember; every undetected polyp escalates the cost of healthcare.

This is where AI has a significant role to play. Using its object recognition capability, AI can identify patterns and is capable of comparing the scanned image against the millions of data inputs from patients around the world. Doctors at Showa University in Yokohama, Japan, were able to scan for polyps with high accuracy. AI-assisted colonoscopy technologies are much more efficient and reliable compared those done by humans alone.

AI systems can also look at more than three hundred features of polyps in less than a second. In an AI-assisted colonoscopy, if a doctor misses a polyp, AI would see it and send an alert so the doctor could go back and take a second look in the same procedure. This dramatically increases the efficiency of scanning and substantially reduces overall healthcare costs by preventing patient readmissions—not to mention the suffering that follows wrong diagnoses. The days are not far off when AI will reach a level of sophistication where it will do colonoscopies with least human intervention.

According to researchers from Massachusetts General Hospital in Boston, AI can be used to accurately detect kidney stones. This research is using CT scans aided by AI to detect a stone. They also trained a neural network to characterize the stone for easy management. AI has shown an amazing 90 percent accuracy both in detection and composition analysis. This substantially increases the efficiency of the procedure. AI can even predict the likelihood of having a kidney stone again in the future, further reducing the healthcare cost of readmission as patients can take preventive steps.

Scientists at Stanford University created an AI diagnosis algorithm for skin cancer using a Google-provided public application programming interface—a set of routines, protocols, and tools for building software and applications. They made a database of nearly 130,000 skin disease images and trained their algorithm to visually diagnose potential cancer.

The algorithm was tested against twenty-one board-certified dermatologists. In its diagnoses of skin lesions, which represented the most common and deadliest skin cancers, the algorithm matched the performance of dermatologists, with a whopping 91 percent accuracy rate. Here again higher efficiency, less doctor time, and fewer wrong diagnoses would cut healthcare costs considerably.

AI is establishing itself in all specialties of healthcare. Below are few unique illustrations to show how AI affects the cost of healthcare while also threatening healthcare jobs, an inevitable collateral damage.

Robots in Surgery

Have you seen a da Vinci surgical robot in action on YouTube? It's amazing to watch how a robot can operate on a human being. Though human surgeons are still needed, the surgical procedure itself is robot-intensive. Surgeons have moved away from the operating table to nearby control stations where they control the operating robots the way players control video games. The surgeons use their surgical knowledge, which is complemented by the precision cutting and stitching done by the machine.

There are many companies competing in the field of robotic surgery, but Intuitive's da Vinci was the first to become well-established in the market.

Robotic surgery provides patients with less discomfort and has quicker recovery time, so the technology reduces hospital costs by shortening hospital stays; there are also fewer readmissions after the procedures, which lead to reduced overall healthcare cost. As of now robot-surgery is used for colorectal, gynecological, head, neck, thoracic, and urological procedures. Between 2004 and 2013 robots performed about 1.7 million surgical procedures, with about 450,000 done during 2012 alone in the United States.

AI Intervention in Robotic Surgery

Although robotic surgery appears to be highly advanced, AI influence is still very minimal. It is still a human-controlled procedure. Many surgeons today are being trained to use the technology and medical students go through residency and fellowship programs that focus on robotic surgery. As time goes on it's possible that some machine-trained doctors might have less developed manual skills since the machine does the actual cutting and suturing.

Surgery robots are just hard-coded robots that function as programmed. They lack a brain. The brain is still the human surgeon. But AI by definition has the potential to intercede. There are many areas where AI is already intervening to make human surgeons more efficient: advanced suturing techniques, accuracy and precision of the surgical movements, better touch and feedback for the surgeon, better visualization of the patient's anatomy, etc., all of which will increase surgical efficiency and eventually reduce costs. Because many of these are still in the research stage, the real AI arms race has yet to begin.

A Johns Hopkins University research team developed a robotic surgical system called the smart tissue autonomous robot (STAR) that can integrate 3-D imaging and sensors to help guide the robot through the suturing process.

Google has teamed up with Johnson and Johnson to develop a robotic surgical device that uses AI to identify human anatomy. This is a game changer in the field of surgery. It may not help a well-versed surgeon but greatly helps new doctors during their training. And as these young, robotic surgeons progress into the future, they will depend more heavily on the technologies they have been trained with. As AI evolves it will ease out the hardcoded robotic technology into more flexible self-learning, adaptable systems.

There are many technical challenges for robotic surgery. It's a fact that all machines are prone to failure. Many things can go wrong with machines during surgery. And robotic devices are vulnerable to hacking. What if these robots were compromised during a critical surgical operation? Many technologies—like blockchain used in bitcoin—that are hard to hack and more reliable are slowly entering healthcare market to improve security.

Robotic surgery also brings up questions of liability. Who is liable for a failed surgery? All the stakeholders including the hospital, equipment manufacturer, software vendor, and surgeon could be involved in the legal tussle. Already Intuitive Inc. has faced a number of product liability lawsuits.

In spite of all these challenges, what will drive this technology is its benefits for patients who will recover more quickly with fewer costs. As AI replaces doctors at the surgical table, the cost of health care will undoubtedly plummet.

Although this looks like a threat to the surgical profession, it's a great opportunity for new jobs and careers to support the new technology. Highly-skilled professionals will be needed to build and manage AI surgical systems. A new field called medical engineering is already evolving, which requires knowledge of both medicine and engineering. In the future, even though we may not see surgeons at the operating table, highly skilled medical engineers will be working behind the scenes developing and monitoring surgical robots making them more intelligent.

Using AI to Detect Tuberculosis

Researchers at Thomas Jefferson University Hospital in Philadelphia are training AI to detect tuberculosis (TB). They are using two models—AlexNet and GoogLeNet— to identify TB on chest X-rays. The findings are published in the Journal of Radiology. AI is learning from a host of medical images to interpret radiographs for the presence of TB. This will have a huge positive impact especially in underdeveloped nations where there are shortages of physicians. According to the World Health Organization, in 2016 about ten million people fell ill from TB, causing 1.8 million deaths. These kinds of fully automated technologies will substantially bring down the cost of healthcare.

AI to Detect Brain Bleeds

IBM Watson and Israel-based MedyMatch Technology are coming together to use AI to help doctors detect brain bleeds resulting from head trauma and stroke. It uses machine learning algorithms that have access to machine vision and patient data to highlight areas of potential presence of cerebral bleeds. According to the American Stroke Association, stroke is the fourth leading cause of death and at the same time one of the top preventable disabilities in the United States.

If you look at all these examples, AI is has big role to play in making them efficient and as a consequence reducing the healthcare cost. New technologies have the potential to rise the healthcare cost while AI has the potential to bring it down. Having said that, it makes sense to incorporate AI in new technologies at an early stage in their development so that the cost can be kept at bay. Good news is many startups are moving in that direction.

Many startups in healthcare are well ahead of the game. They are already incorporating AI in their products and services. A great way to start to survive the competition. This undoubtedly is threatening the traditional laid back healthcare businesses who are now forced to adapt AI. Below are a few examples.

The startup, BrainQ, is developing an AI to customize treatment protocols for people who cannot walk because of a stroke, spinal trauma, or brain injuries.

Another startup Byteflies is developing a plug-n-play platform for wearables to convert raw data into meaningful data so anyone can use it.

Cytovale's vision technology looks at how a cell transforms when a patient gets infected with sepsis, helping in the early detection of sepsis.

The other critical aspect in all the above examples is that AI needs enormous amounts of data to function effectively be it diagnostics or procedure. It means that the more data we collect from the human body, the better it is for AI to function efficiently and bring down the cost of healthcare.

Human Body Big Data

When you go to a doctor with symptoms of an ailment, diagnosis begins with some questions. Then the doctor could check you physically and may also order lab tests. Once those results arrive, the doctor will analyze them using their medical knowledge to arrive at the best diagnosis.

If you look at this routine process in a pragmatic way, a medical diagnosis is nothing but analytics of human body big data . Here the word *data* means patient symptoms, patient lab results, the doctor's medical knowledge and past experiences in treating similar ailments, etc. If the doctor has not treated an ailment before then, their academic knowledge is the only valuable resource.

Every time there is a new medical breakthrough, the doctors will learn about it from medical journals or attending conferences. Every time a new ailment is treated, the doctor's knowledge enhances. Every time the doctor misdiagnoses, they will learn from the mistakes. There is a constant learning process in medicine that leads to more reliable diagnoses over time. It's this learning process that AI is challenging.

Today medical knowledge is digitally available online and in journals, books, and publications. Doctors' experiences are now being digitally recorded in all hospitals in the form of electronic medical records (EMR), a huge database of varied data both in ethnicity and demography. Every time there is a research breakthrough, the medical knowledge will be immediately available in digital publications. Every time a new ailment is treated it shows up on a patient's EMR. There is a constant update of digital information in real time.

Before the digital revolution, a doctor's experiences stayed in their memory, with only a fraction making it to journals and books. There's an obvious advantage of having that information instantly available in a digital format. The human element that stored that information is slowly becoming obsolete. This is a significant development in medicine.

Further, if there is an outbreak of a disease or a medical research breakthrough, instantly the information gets digitized.

This kind of massive digital data is giving way to telemedicine – a relatively new concept, a unique way of providing clinical care from a distance. This is especially a life saver for rural communities. Although it is still being used for distance care, it is now slowly becoming mainstream as it offers convenience of getting healthcare from the comforts of home. Many telemedicine companies offer 24/7 access to on-call doctor, virtual visits, mobile access so patients can track their health. All this is feasible mainly because of digitization of medical data and AI to do the analytics.

With mountains of digital data, it is too overwhelming for human doctors to handle. AI intervention in healthcare is very natural. At some point in the future, it becomes inevitable for doctors to use AI in every medical diagnosis and procedure to make them more efficient and cost-effective.

The *next big thing* in healthcare undoubtedly is the evolution of devices that capture human body big data in real time. There is already a name for it: digital therapeutics. This is a fast-growing field both for job opportunities and entrepreneurship, all geared towards paring down healthcare costs.

AI in Digital Therapeutics

One of the leading digital therapy devices making news today are pills with ingestible embedded sensors that can tell patients and doctors whether a medication has been taken properly? In November 2017 the FDA approved Abilify MyCite (aripiprazole tablets with sensors). The sensor in the pill sends a message to a wearable patch when the medication is taken. The patch then transmits the information to a mobile app so that patients can track the ingestion of the medication on their smartphone. They can also permit their doctors and nurses to access the information. This is especially great for patients with dementia or mental illness, and surely this will evolve for regular patients who can't keep track of medication because of busy work schedules. Better patient management improves their health, resulting in reduced healthcare costs.

For certain people with diabetes, the biggest innovation may be Dexcom's sensor, which displays glucose data on the mobile phone. A Dexcom sensor with a hair-thin wire is placed just under the skin. A transmitter clips to it and sends glucose data via Bluetooth to the Dexcom receiver and then to an iPhone. Even though this device has limitations, with diabetes on the rise, we could expect more investment to go into the monitoring of blood sugar, which will advance the technology behind preventive healthcare.

The other devices that are becoming popular are asthma inhalers that connect to the cloud and captures local air-quality data to provide personalized feedback to patients. The Australian company Adherium has come up with a monitoring device for AstraZeneca's Symbicort aerosol inhaler, dubbed the SmartTouch. And Propeller Health in partnership with GlaxoSmithKline has come out with a sensor-enabled inhaler to monitor usage and provide biofeedback. This history of patient medication data helps physicians make evidence-based decisions and greatly helps healthcare cost-reduction programs.

Smart devices that are health tracking wearables like Fitbit are popular across the world. Most of these devices are able to track running speed and distance with GPS capability, step count, swimming stroke count, calorie count, etc. Some also have a heart rate monitor, and sleep tracker that can analyze sleep patterns and recovery.

All these sensing devices are innately IOTs feeding data to AI-driven apps in phones that helps patients track their own health, reducing doctor visits while at the same time doctors use the data of patients more efficiently, reducing hospital readmissions and eventually reducing costs.

IoTs and RFIDs to Improve Operational Efficiency in Hospitals

Have you heard of doctors operating on wrong patients or wrong part of the body? In busy hospitals, errors are bound to happen. These mistakes not only escalate the cost of healthcare but cause painful suffering and even death. Many hospitals are already adopting RFID tags in bracelets to identify patients and get all the patient information.

Consider a nurse giving medication to a patient. At the patient's bedside they can use a mobile computer to scan the patient's ID bracelet to confirm the patient's name and date of birth and to bring up their medical record. The computer will provide a guided workflow with any instructions for administering drugs, underpinning the five "rights" of medicine administration— the right patient, the right drug, the right dose, the right route, and the right time. The nurse can also scan the barcode on the drug packet to cross-check that the patient has no allergy to it. The computer is then used to confirm that the medication has been taken, with a note auto-created on the patient's EMR. This kinds of improvement in operational efficiency would greatly reduce healthcare costs.

Effect of Junk Food on Healthcare Costs

Junk food has literally changed the food habits of an entire generation of humans, resulting in obesity, diabetes, and other long-term health issues at very young ages around the world. Even for people who eat healthy food, it's not always possible to keep track of the calorie, especially when eating out. We are all just eating blind. The effects of blind-eating are slow to manifest, and many people only notice a health condition like obesity or diabetes or heart disease after years or even decades.

The reason for eating blindly is the lack of digital therapeutics. With digital data coming out of human body, we will soon be able to make better choices about what we eat, which will cut healthcare costs. This brings the food and healthcare industry much closer and they may influence each other. It wouldn't be a surprise in the near future to see a customized menu appearing on our mobile phones as soon as we enter a restaurant. The built-in AI systems will decide what is best for us. The restaurants may use that data and prepare a customized entrée just for us. It all means one thing: in the future the restaurants will prepare food keeping their customers' health in mind.

The Dark Side of AI

Amidst all the exciting news, there is a dark side to these disruptive technologies. They are forcing doctors to learn new skills to use AI software. Those who can't or won't adopt the new technology might see their career stall. Nursing and other supporting personnel including hospital administration jobs are experiencing similar challenges.

Futurists are predicting massive physician unemployment at the hands of technology while the American Association of Medical Colleges predicts a physician shortfall of about 95,000 over the next decade. These predictions seem contradictory because employment shortages and unemployment scenarios are normally mutually exclusive. However, in healthcare they can coexist. Physician shortages occur because of the impact of technology. Any physician or surgeon who cannot adapt to technology—usually those who are older—will be the ones most affected and they may retire prematurely, thus causing both physician shortage and unemployment at the same time. Physician shortages significantly affect the cost of healthcare. It is not hard to visualize that very soon we will see hospitals with more young doctors who can cope modern devices, robots, and AI.

Every one of the healthcare technologies discussed above, when swathed in AI, requires less doctor engagement. When these healthcare procedures diverge into more AI and less human-dependent, they will have a modest price tag.

To go from a highly doctor-regimented system to doctor-less system is a unique journey in the sense that no matter how sophisticated the technology is, it's not easy to fully hand over procedures to a machine, even with the support of AI. We are ethically and legally obligated to make sure it is 100 percent safe.

No matter how technologically smart the da Vinci robotic surgery is, it will take a while before it becomes fully doctor-less because obviously human lives are at stake. Healthcare is highly risk-centric, so the evolution of technology in healthcare will be much slower than other non-healthcare technologies. Nonetheless, that transition has begun.

With the arrival of AI, doctors' involvement in diagnosis and procedures is expected to diminish, gradually reducing the cost of healthcare. This will happen procedure by procedure as each one is unique. When AI completely replaces the doctor for a specific procedure, that would then have the potential to become a global product that can be sold at affordable prices. Every healthcare procedure eventually will go thru this tipping point when swaddled with AI.

Strangely enough, we don't know how AI learns. Each AI is unique in its functionality. It is hard to predict at what stage we will begin to trust AI fully in healthcare. But looking at the current developments and wide acceptance of AI, those days are not far off. Healthcare cost contraction may not happen until we begin to adopt more AI in all specialties.

AI is not a healthcare technology; it is just software that is immensely capable of processing large loads of big data to make healthcare more efficient. In the future, new healthcare procedures will inevitably come to market with built-in AI capability to fight market competition.

The doctors should pay close attention to these new AI techniques being developed that will eventually challenge them. Physicians and surgeons of the future have to learn to live with AI by constantly upgrading their skills. Anyone who has difficulty handling AI will be left out. It would be wiser for healthcare professionals to learn AI technologies early in their careers whenever the opportunity arises.

While routine cases and recurring chronic diseases are managed by AI, rare diseases would get the full attention from the research community, taking healthcare to the next level. Traditionally doctors and hospitals have been focusing on recurring illnesses for the revenue. However, in the future when uniqueness becomes the revenue stream, then healthcare will take a new turn. This is a tremendous, exciting entrepreneurial opportunity for doctors, who could work with research companies to market unique clinical data from rare ailments. Doctors could also join hands with software companies to build competing AI software.

There is another upcoming technology that could significantly affect healthcare in many ways. Nanotechnology in medicine is a highly promising technology where nanobots would float in the bloodstream capturing and delivering real-time data. They are also capable of performing repairs at the cellular level and deliver drugs to specific types of cells, such as cancer cells. Any further advances in these techniques could revolutionize the way we detect and treat diseases. The global revenue from nano-enabled products is steadily growing, from $340 billion in 2010 to $730 billion in 2012 and is expected to reach $4 trillion by the end of 2019.

Imagine how efficient it would be during a robotic operation to have nanobots floating in the bloodstream sending vital data about the body. Future surgery could be a combination of robotic surgery from the outside and nanosurgery from inside.

If you look at where healthcare is heading, it all points to the science of data capture from the body and its analytics using AI. Telemedicine, robotic surgery, preventive medicine, nanotechnology, and many other upcoming advances are all craving data for their evolution.

The Wrap Up

With the arrival of AI, doctors' involvement in diagnosis and procedures is expected to diminish, gradually reducing the cost of healthcare. Now imagine the impact of low-cost healthcare on the society. Even the poorest of the poor can afford quality healthcare with their share of UBI.

We are becoming more comfortable talking about unconditional basic income as housing, transportation, food and healthcare have the potential to become significantly cheaper with AI. Our future with AI looks so rich and secure one wonders if we really need to work at all in the future and whether there will be any motivation to do so.

It is understandable poor people struggle hard to make money, but the wealthy who have all the financial security in the world work equally as hard.

Achievement is the secret behind our evolution. A millionaire tries to add one more million to it. A billionaire tries to double it. More money, more power, more fame keeps us busy. Everyone struggles hard to acquire more of everything. In the rich AI future, however, people will have a choice. They can sit doing nothing or work in a high-stress job. If they sit doing nothing and depend on social welfare, they will helplessly watch others progressing in their lives earning more wealth, exclusive recognition, better social status, and enjoying all the great joys of what the world has to offer. Eventually desire wins.

In this book I have done my best to illustrate with real-world examples the possible ways to unleash AI on global warming and at the same time shelter those who lost their jobs to AI. Today's challenge is not just to combat climate change but to survive the inevitable collateral damage.

Unified Voice of AI

The rise of AI is not an accident. With an unprecedented growth in data, human cognitive capabilities like thinking, understanding, learning, and remembering have reached their limitations. AI is rising at the right opportune time. The complexities of fighting global warming is too overwhelming for human cognitive capability. AI's appearance in the market is too obvious.

Although there are numerous businesses and research organizations that are actively using AI, on the surface that is promising, the reality is businesses are currently only using AI as another tool to reduce the overhead cost. There is no dedicated, coordinated effort to build a unified AI to fight global warming.

It would be prudent for global organizations to recognize the importance of AI and apply their resources to developing one master AI that could interact with individual AIs that are fighting global warming in their own arena.

The master AI could become a global data center capturing, storing, and analyzing in real time the incoming big data from around the world and sharing it with other solitary AIs around the globe helping them all become more efficient. Similar concept could be extended to the data captured from reforestation efforts, ocean alkalinity efforts, CCS efforts, and so on, providing invaluable information to research organizations and governments. And above all, having one plan of action from one AI would allow the most efficient use of resources.

Who could build such a master AI? An eminent global organization like IPCC would be the best fit.

With a master AI, global efforts can be easily tracked and measured, allowing informed decisions. If there is any surprising CO2 addition either from an inefficient fossil plant or a forest fire, the master AI would know it immediately because it is provided the global CO2 data in real time.

If there is a reforestation effort, the master AI can figure out how thick the forest would be in next few years and its effect on CO2 content. With data coming from IoTs, it could extrapolate any changes in rain pattern and how it affects the trees' growth. Many reforestation efforts have failed globally because they lacked adequate, timely information—a problem a network of AIs solves.

The idea of a master AI that shares information might prompt concerns over intellectual property. But it should be viewed as a great opportunity for businesses and research organizations to license their technologies, if they wish, for royalties.

As time progresses, as the cost of carbon comes down, all the carbon-based products will become less expensive, increasing their market demand, which in turn would drive the carbon capturing ventures. It's not enough just having a master AI; it's equally important that we have a massive proliferation of solitary AIs in all areas of global warming for the master AI to function proficiently. Right now we have enough solitary AIs around the world to lay the foundation for that mighty master AI.

With a global network of AIs at its disposal, the master AI will become an invaluable ally in our fight against global warming.

How Can We All Pitch in?

Although it may seem impossible to defeat such a mighty beast like global warming at individual level, we all can pitch in by embracing AI, honing our hi-tech skills and becoming part of the technological evolution. The fight against global warming will transpire seamlessly as long as we are skilled enough.

Any resistance to adapting AI and other new technologies will only make global businesses and global economies stunted. Furthermore, the technological advancement within businesses will slow to a halt if there isn't a skilled workforce to hire. And that is where we are heading now. That need to change. We as individuals can make it happen.

Many people love the status quo of their jobs and their lives, and refuse to learn new technical skills or change the way they operate. They are incontestably hindering the fight against global warming. Realistically, in this fight, we should either be the driving force as entrepreneurs or at least a supporting force as skilled employees, but definitely not a dragging force as unskilled laborers.

Employees who are left behind in the world of AI, are not alone. Every one of us will pass through this difficult stage of helplessness at some point in our lives. Some will adapt sooner, and some will be forced to adapt later. Those who reinvent themselves and learn the skills necessary to thrive in this tech-based economy will survive in the workforce for a longer time. They are the missing link in our fight against global warming.

Acknowledgements

Grateful acknowledgment is made many international organizations having provided useful quality data for public research. They include organizations like World Health Organization, National Center for Public Policy and Higher Education, www.ipcc.ch, www.House.gov, www.cbo.gov, www.eia.doe.gov, www.nasa.gov, www.ers.usda.gov, stanford.edu, forbes.com, ibm.com, dhs.gov, industry40summit.com, darpa.mil, epa.gov, nature.org, and www.cms.gov.

There are several groups of people to whom I am very thankful for their help and advice. Many thanks to reviewers including Kirkus reviews, Clarion reviews and Kathleen Tracy for her valuable advice and feedback. And thanks to my family and friends for their helpful comments, advice, and support.

Bibliography

"Aerosols and Incoming Sunlight (Direct Effects)."
NASA Observatory. November 2, 2010.
https://earthobservatory.nasa.gov/Features/Aeros
ols/page3.php

"Artificial Intelligence Replaces Physicists." The
Australian National University. Last modified May
16, 2016. http://www.anu.edu.au/news/all-
news/artificial-intelligence-replaces-physicists

"Artificial Intelligence Takes on the Stock Market." BBC
(video). 01:21. February 10, 2016.
http://www.bbc.com/news/av/technology-
35405336/artificial-intelligence-takes-on-the-stock-
market

"Artificial Intelligence." Wikipedia. Accessed July 12,
2018.
https://en.wikipedia.org/wiki/Artificial_intelligenc
e

"Atmospheric Aerosols: What Are They, and Why Are
They So Important?" Bob Allen (ed.). NASA. Last
modified August 7, 2017.
https://www.nasa.gov/centers/langley/news/facts
heets/Aerosols.html

Baker, David R. "Robots Cut Solar Construction Costs."
San Francisco Chronicle. June 17, 2013.
https://www.sfchronicle.com/business/article/Ro
bots-cut-solar-construction-costs-4604343.php

"Beijing Uses Machine Learning and Big Data to Target
    Pollution Controls." Apolitical. Accessed July 12,
    2018. https://apolitical.co/solution_article/beijing-
    uses-machine-learning-big-data-target-pollution-
    controls/

Bohannon, John. "A New Breed of Scientist, with
    Brains of Silicon." *Science*. July 5, 2017..
    http://www.sciencemag.org/news/2017/07/new-
    breed-scientist-brains-silicon

Callaghan, Greg. "Can Swarms of Seed-Bearing Drones
    Help Regrow the Planet's Forests?" *Sydney Morning
    Herald*. August 26, 2017.
    https://www.smh.com.au/lifestyle/can-swarms-of-
    seedbearing-drones-help-regrow-the-planets-
    forests-20170823-gy2ei5.html

"Carbon Capture and Storage." Exxonmobil. Accessed
    July 12, 2018.
    http://corporate.exxonmobil.com/en/technology/
    carbon-capture-and-storage

"Carbon Capture and Storage." Wikipedia. Accessed July
    13, 2018.
    https://en.wikipedia.org/wiki/Carbon_capture_and
    _storage

"Carbon Capture and the Future of Coal Power." NRG.
    Accessed July 12, 2018 https://www.nrg.com/case-
    studies/petra-nova.html

"Carbon Dioxide 101." National Energy Technology
    Laboratory. Accessed July 13, 2018.

https://www.netl.doe.gov/research/coal/carbon-storage/carbon-storage-faqs/what-are-the-primary-sources-of-co2

"Carbon Dioxide in Earth's Atmosphere." Wikipedia. Accessed July 13, 2018. https://en.wikipedia.org/wiki/Carbon_dioxide_in_Earth%27s_atmosphere

"Carbon Footprint Calulator." Environmental Protection Agency. Accessed July 13, 2018. https://www3.epa.gov/carbon-footprint-calculator/

"Carbon Sequestration." Lamont-Doherty Earth Observatory. Accessed July 12, 2018. http://www.ldeo.columbia.edu/gpg/projects/carbon-sequestration

"Carbon Sink." Wikipedia. Accessed July 13, 2018. https://en.wikipedia.org/wiki/Carbon_sink

Clark, Jen. "What Is the Internet of Things?" Internet of Things Blog. November 17, 2016. https://www.ibm.com/blogs/ Internet-of-things/what-is-the-iot/

Conway, Erik. "What's in a Name? Global Warming vs. Climate Change Global." NASA. Accessed July 12, 2018. https://www.nasa.gov/topics/earth/features/climate_by_any_other_name.html

"DARPA Robotics Challenge (DRC) (Archived)." Defense Advanced Research Projects Agency.

Accessed July 13, 2018.
https://www.darpa.mil/program/darpa-robotics-challenge

"Deep Convective Clouds and Chemistry Experiment (DC3)." The National Center for Atmospheric Research. Accessed July 12, 2018. https://www2.acom.ucar.edu/dc3

"Deep Thunder Now Hyper-Local on a Global Scale." IBM (blog). June 15, 2016. https://www.ibm.com/blogs/research/2016/06/deep-thunder-now-hyper-local-global/

"eMotion Butterflies." Festo. Accessed July 13, 2018. https://www.festo.com/group/en/cms/10216.htm

"Global Climate Change: Vital Signs of the Planet." NASA. Accessed July 13, 2018. https://climate.nasa.gov/vital-signs/carbon-dioxide/

Hansen, James, Makiko Sato, Pushker Kharecha, and Karina von Schuckmann "Earth's Energy Imbalance." NASA Goddard Institute for Space Studies. January 2012. https://www.giss.nasa.gov/research/briefs/hansen_16/

http://carbonengineering.com/

http://www.predpol.com/

http://www.shotspotter.com/

https://globalthermostat.com/

https://stanleyinnovation.com

https://us.hikvision.com/en

https://www.ibm.com

https://www.industry40summit.com/2018-programme/

https://www.kavout.com/

https://www.nature.org/greenliving/carboncalculator/i
    ndex.htm

https://www.research.ibm.com/green-
    horizons/interactive

https://www.transcriptic.com/ "Internet of Things."
    Wikipedia. Accessed July 12, 2018.
    https://en.wikipedia.org/wiki/Internet_of_things

"IPCC Fourth Assessment Report: Climate Change
    2007." Intergovernmental Panel on Climate Change.
    Accessed July 13, 2018.
    https://www.ipcc.ch/publications_and_data/ar4/w
    g1/en/ch7s7-3-2-2.html

Kumar, Vijay. "The Future of Flying Objects." Ted
    Talks (video). 13:10. April 2015.
    https://www.ted.com/talks/vijay_kumar_the_futur
    e_of_flying_robots

Mahtanim, Shibani and Zusha Elinson. "Artificial
    Intelligence Could Soon Enhance Real-Time Police
    Surveillance." *Wall Street Journal.* Last modified April
    3, 2018. https://www.wsj.com/articles/artificial-
    intelligence-could-soon-enhance-real-time-police-
    surveillance-1522761813

Marr, Bernard. "What Is the Difference Between
    Artificial Intelligence and Machine Learning?"
    Forbes. December 6, 2016. https://www.forbes.com

McCarthy, John. "What Is AI?/Basic Questions."
    Accessed July 12, 2018.
    http://jmc.stanford.edu/artificial-intelligence/what-
    is-ai/index.html

"NOAA to Develop New Global Weather Model."
    National Oceanic and Atmospheric Administration.
    July 27, 2016. http://www.noaa.gov/media-
    release/noaa-to-develop-new-global-weather-model

O'Reilly, Lara. "A Japanese Ad Agency Invented an AI
    Creative Director—and Ad Execs Preferred Its Ad
    to a Human's." *Business Insider*. March 12, 2917.
    http://www.businessinsider.com/mccann-japans-
    ai-creative-director-creates-better-ads-than-a-
    human-2017-3

"Quest Carbon Capture and Storage." Shell Canada.
    Accessed July 12, 2018.
    https://www.shell.ca/en_ca/about-us/projects-
    and-sites/quest-carbon-capture-and-storage-
    project.html

"Radio Frequency Identification (RFID): What Is It?"
    Department of Homeland Security. Last modified
    July 6, 2009. https://www.dhs.gov/radio-
    frequency-identification-rfid-what-it

"Radio-Frequency Identification." Wikipedia. Accessed July 12, 2018. https://en.wikipedia.org/wiki/Radio-frequency_identification

"Safely Storing Carbon Dioxide." Chevron. Accessed July 12, 2018. https://www.chevron.com/stories/safely-storing-co2

Shaw, Darren. "How Wimbledon Is Using IBM Watson AI to Power Highlights, Analytics and Enriched Fan Experiences." IBM. July 6, 2017. https://www.ibm.com/blogs/watson/2017/07/ibm-watsons-ai-is-powering-wimbledon-highlights-analytics-and-a-fan-experiences/

Smith, John R. "IBM Research Takes Watson to Hollywood with the First Cognitive Movie Trailer." IBM Think Blog. August 31, 2016. https://www.ibm.com/blogs/think/2016/08/cognitive-movie-trailer/

"Solar Radiation Management." Wikipedia. Accessed July 13, 2018. https://en.wikipedia.org/wiki/Solar_radiation_management

"Sophia." Hanson Robotics. Accessed July 12, 2018. http://www.hansonrobotics.com/robot/sophia/

"The New Carbon Economy." CO2 Solutions. Accessed July 12, 2018. https://www.co2solutions.com/

"Tomra's Mineral and Ore Sorting Equipment for More
Profit." Tomra. Accessed July 13, 2018.
https://www.tomra.com/en/sorting/mining

"Trends in Atmospheric Carbon Dioxide." Earth
System Research Laboratory. Accessed July 13,
2018.
https://www.esrl.noaa.gov/gmd/ccgg/trends/gl_d
ata.html

Walker, Jon. "Chatbot Comparison: Facebook,
Microsoft, Amazon, and Google." Telemergence.
March 29, 2018.
https://www.techemergence.com/chatbot-
comparison-facebook-microsoft-amazon-google/

"What Is Carbon Dioxide Removal and Why Is It
Important?" Climeworks. Accessed July 12, 2018.
http://www.climeworks.com/co2-removal/

"What is CCS?" Carbon Capture and Storage
Association. Accessed July 13,
2018.http://www.ccsassociation.org/what-is-ccs/

"What Is SRM?" Solar Radiation Management
Governance Initiative. Accessed July 13, 2018.
http://www.srmgi.org/what-is-srm

Index

3

3-D printing, *93, 97*

    housing, *98*

    how it works, *97*

    manufacturing, *98*

    using IoTs, *101, 102, 103, 104*

A

AI for Earth, *64*

albedo, *62*

Amazon Go, *29*

artificial intelligence

    career opportunities, *46*

    definition, *14*

    dependency on IoTs, 24

    health care, *131*

    healthcare, *132*

    in law enforcement, *36*

    in marketing, 35

    in moviemaking, *29*

    in sports, *30*

    in surgery, *135*

    job loss, *146*

    mining, *37*

    personnel recruitment, *39*

    predictive models, *33*

    security surveillance, *34*

    stocl market, *41*

    threats to, *45*

    tunnel drilling, *122*

    weather forecasting, 33

automated cooking, *125*

autonomous technology, *106,*

    107, 108, 109

    commuting, *110*

    job creation, *113*

    self-driving cars, *112*

    taxis, *112*

B

big data, 19, 20, 26

Blue River Technology, *126*

C

carbon budget, *57*

carbon chart, *52*

carbon dioxide, *51*

    absorption, *55*

    artificial capture, *74*

    cap-and-trade, *78*

    capture, *75*

    direct air capture, *79*

    natural capture, *70*

    sources of, *53*

carbon sink, *54*

chatbots, *30, 31*

Chef Watson, *127*

Climeworks, *80, 162*

CO2 fertilization effect, *56*

D

data analytics, *20, 31, 138*

digital therapeutics, *140, 145*

digital therapy devices, *140*

disruptive technologies, *94, 145*

E

electronic medical records, *139*

G

geoengineering, *62, 65, 66, 69, 90, 91*

global warming, *9, 10, 11, 24, 48, 50, 51, 52, 54, 55, 56, 57, 59, 60, 62, 68, 83, 90, 105, 150, 151*

Green Horizon Project, *64*

H

high-speed transport, **116**, **118**, **121**, **124**

human-generated data, *21*

hyperloop, *118*, *119*, *120*, *121*, *122*

Hyperloop Pod Competition, *118*, *119*

I

Internet of Things

definition, *22*

in healthcare, *25*

smart devices, *23*, *24*

J

job loss, *93*, *128*

K

Kavout. *See* stock market

Kumar, Vijay, *44*

L

Liquid Robotics, *71*

M

machine-generated data, *21*

manufacturing, *38*, *94*

Musk, Elon, *118*

N

nanotechnology, *149*

neural net, 17, 18, 19

P

product delivery, *32*

R

radio frequency identification (RFID), 26

definition, *26*

how it works, *26*

security issues, 28

rapid research, *64, 67, 68*

reforestation, *72*

robot ant tunneling, *123*

robotic surgery, *135*

robots, 31, 38, 42, 43, 44, 45, 67,

68, 71, 72, 77, 84, 85, 86, 87,

91, 93, 101, 102, 113, 122,

135, 146, 159

disaster response, *43*

S

self-driving cars, *107, 108, 112,*

114

ShotSpotter, *36*

smart labels in healthcare, *143*

solar energy, *82, 84*

Sophia, 35, 162

T

Tomra, *126, See* mining

U

universal basic income, *95*

V

Virgin Hyperloop One, *120*

W

Watson, *29, 30, 37, 127, 136,*

161

wireless body area networks,

143

Z

Zymergen, *77*